A philosopher's
take on
economics

second edition

T0308050

A philosopher's take on

economics

second edition

John Tippett

SHEPHEARD-WALWYN
PUBLISHERS

First published in 2013 by
Delphian Books, a division of
New Frontier Creative Services Pty Ltd
1/29 Mile End Road
Rouse Hill, NSW 2155 Australia
61-2 8625 5530

Second Edition 2021
British Library Cataloguing in Publication Data
A catalogue record of this book
is available from the British Library

ISBN 978-08-5683-540-7

Typeset by RefineCatch Ltd, Bungay, Suffolk

Printed and bound in the United Kingdom
by 4edge Limited

FOREWORD

I enjoyed reading *A Philosopher's Take on Economics,* for three reasons. First, as the author asserts, it is a book premised on first principles. There is no necessity for the reader to have an understanding of the works of economic history or of the latest journal articles in economics. Instead, it is a work based on the common sense of an observer of the economic system, using simple examples which illustrate the importance of economics in human decision-making.

Secondly, it addresses the question of the social relevance of economics, a question that has been subordinated by modern economic theory. There is more discussion of economic freedom and economic justice than in the average volume on economics; as there should be. It is, in many ways, a philosophical lamentation, best summarised in the last chapter, where the author asserts "maybe, just maybe, the real problem, the real immediate concern is philosophy, specifically the lack of it in the lives of individuals, communities and nations!" My only divergence from this statement is that I would replace maybe with certainly. Philosophy is essential to the study of our economic lives.

Thirdly, this book has coverage; it returns to what economics is about. Economics is not about measuring artificial constructs such as GDP, or inflation, nor whether stock prices follow a geometric brownian motion. Economics concerns human welfare, and the best mechanism to achieve the fairest outcome which preserves our civilisation. That cannot be achieved without a portfolio which covers all the components of the economic system.

Dr Kim Sawyer
August 2012

CONTENTS

ACKNOWLEDGEMENTS

This book owes its existence in large part to the influence of four remarkable men – three of whom I have met personally and thereby became acquainted with their thought and stature; the fourth, Henry George (1839–1897), through his writings.

First, Henry George. I became acquainted with Henry George through his seminal work *Progress and Poverty* (1879), which informed and uplifted my thought forever; particularly as it followed upon a lengthy, gruelling period of exacting academic study of economics that had left me with much frustration and little economic knowledge of any value.

Second, Leon MacLaren (1910–1993). I met Mr MacLaren both in person and through his magnificent three-year course in economics – based on Henry George – which I had the great privilege of delivering to dedicated students of the School of Philosophy in Melbourne for a period of almost twenty years. Delivering Leon MacLaren's course had a profound effect on refining and giving direction to the "rough-hewn" formulation of the subject that had formed in my mind upon becoming acquainted with *Progress and Poverty*.

Third, Mr John Jepsen, Leader of the School of Philosophy in Melbourne. Mr Jepsen provided on-going and unfaltering encouragement and support for the conduct of those economics courses; and, indeed, it has been as a result of his life of extraordinary sacrifice that the School of Philosophy became established in Melbourne in the first place. Without this School there would, of course, have been no economics groups at all and no exposure to the work of Leon MacLaren.

Fourth, Dr Kim Sawyer, former professor of finance and economics at the University of Melbourne and now my friend. For fifteen years or thereabouts Dr Sawyer has been a constant source of inspiration through his brilliance of mind, his acute perception of what really matters in economics, and, importantly, through his person and his friendship and the high value he places on virtuous behaviour.

I have a deep sense of gratitude to all of these four extraordinary men.

I am apprehensive about the title of this book. It may convey the implication that I consider myself to be a philosopher; that is to say, it may convey the implication that "I really think I know something!". This is far from the truth. Whilst I have been a member of the School of Philosophy in Melbourne for more than 40 years this period of contact has always been strictly in the capacity of *student* of this wonderful subject, not master. However, being a student of practical philosophy for a considerable period of time, coupled with a natural interest in economics that began to show itself in my late 'teens, allows for a different perspective on economics – a "philosophical perspective". *This* is the reason for the title of the book, *not* any pretensions of being a philosopher.

This second edition includes (in chapter 10) a consideration of the hurtful, destructive effects of shutting down an economy; and further discussion of the intimate relationship between philosophy and economics.

The major message of the book is perennial. It is aimed at presenting a common-sense, first-principles, philosophical perspective on a vital subject that seems to have lost its way. There *is* such a thing as justice, there *is* such a thing as truth; and these two need not be lost forever.

John Tippett

August 2020

INTRODUCTION

It is not uncommon to find that when something of major consequence in human life goes wrong, a simple matter but a matter of fundamental importance and far-reaching effect has been ignored. Such is the story of economics. It takes no keen observation whatsoever to see that twenty-first century economic affairs, right across the world, are in a mess. The cost of housing – one of mankind's most basic needs – has risen to such crippling heights that stories emerge of people living out of their cars or out of caravans. The cost of living – the cost of simply remaining alive – has risen to such an extent that few families with only one income survive without enduring hardship. Unemployment is common; and troubling health conditions that are related to living under economic stress are the lot of far too many of our fellow human beings.

This book is a treatise on economics, viewed from a philosophical perspective. It is a philosophically oriented examination of the *first principles* of the subject – the foundation principles, upon which the whole economic fabric has grown and rests. As is the case with all principles, detailed ramifications arise when applied in *practice*. A full discussion of the workings out of these ramifications is for another occasion.

The intention of life itself is that all may *have* it, and have it more abundantly. Economics is the knowledge that makes this possible. It exists to allow people to live together in communities in which *all* members may enjoy prosperity, well-being, harmony, creativity, and the opportunity to take and develop responsibility. Life is meant for the well-being of *all* who are born onto this earth – not just for the few, not just for the privileged, not just for those who are lucky. The purpose of economics is to show *how* mankind may live together in communities, in prosperity, unfettered by the strictures of necessity. It is to show how mankind may be *set free* economically. The real purpose, the ideal, of human life is that it is the opportunity to perfect individual human nature, and a life lived under economic freedom makes this ideal a practical possibility.

Economic freedom engenders a sense of connectedness between people. Life is not meant to be a cruel struggle and it is not meant to be a game of fierce competition; rather, an exercise of co-operation. Nature is generous; there is plenty for all. Whilst the notion of scarcity is a foundation principle of contemporary economics textbooks, scarcity really exists only in relation to greed, it is a consequence of greed. Further, economics is an aspect of law – that law necessary to bring about justice in the transactions between people living and working in society. Hence, in the first instance and therefore of high significance, economics is intimately concerned with human nature – the nature of those who live and work.

There are several aspects of human nature that are of vital importance to economics. First, it is an observable fact that human beings are naturally gregarious. We desire the company of our fellow human beings, and choose to live in communities rather than in isolation. This desire to live in communities has important implications for the natural resource, land – in particular its site value. Consideration of this value and its cause is a fundamental tenet for any understanding of economics.

Second, it is natural to work. It is in the very nature of every man and woman to want to work. The human being is born into this world with a purpose to fulfil. The way this purpose manifests – the way it makes itself known, or felt – is that we desire satisfaction or happiness. It is in search of satisfaction that the human being works, and this satisfaction may be sought at the physical or mental levels, usually both. Thus mankind, individually and collectively, has needs and wants that give rise to the desire for their fulfilment; *and* is equipped to meet these desires by way of productive work. Hence, being employed is a natural consequence of the very act of existence. Correspondingly, because nobody is without needs and wants, and no able-bodied human being is without the means of doing something towards meeting them, unemployment is an impossibility (except these needs and wants be entirely ignored or denied and the individual thereby dies). With few exceptions everyone wants to do something, and this means that forced, or involuntary, unemployment is an artificial phenomenon. Whilst the amount, type and refinement of work varies considerably between individuals, the great majority have an innate desire to work; laziness and sloth are just a temporary suppression of this desire. There is just one proviso: there must be open and ready access to the natural resources necessary for work to take place.

Third, mankind is born onto the surface of an earth teeming with raw materials – natural resources – the very things that are required for meeting human needs. This situation is self-existent; it does not have to be created. The raw materials only require being worked upon in order to fashion them into a form suitable for human use. The human being gives them – the raw materials – suitable expression.

Hence, the fundamental premises of economics are simple and in no way artificial or contrived. The job of the economist is to remove entirely any incentives *not* to work, and to provide the "rules", the law, by which, firstly, access to necessary naturally occurring resources is obtained, and secondly, production is distributed. The single and often-proclaimed policy aim of increasing production (that is, of economic *growth*) is not sufficient, because the question of distribution remains. Both production and justice in its distribution are important, not just production.

Finally, with respect to human nature, it needs to be noted that satiety is not the aim of economics and is not the aim of life. Full and substantial well-being is the aim of life, and attempts to satisfy unbridled human desire – any and all whims and fancies without regard to reason or measure – do not lead to this. The economist needs to know this, and in knowing this will appreciate that the earth's resources *are* sufficient to meet all needs but probably not sufficient to meet all unbridled desires. Full and substantial happiness does not lie in the direction of satiety. But nor can it be expected to prevail where basic needs of human life are denied. This is only being reasonable, and proper economics is most reasonable.

A broad appreciation of the relevant aspects of human nature is essential to any intelligent consideration of economics. Economics, like other branches of learning, is a resource to be applied toward the enactment of proper and civilised human life. Humankind is its subject, and its purpose is to establish and maintain justice between people in their economic relationships. If this is forgotten then economics degenerates into a plethora of segregated concerns over exchange rates, interest rates, inflation rates and all sorts of other rates, all of which are of some relevance but *not as ends in themselves.* They are tools to be used in the management of an economy. But if the prime place and importance of the human being is overlooked; that is to say, if it be ignored or forgotten that economics is concerned with the prosperity and well-being of people – *all* people – then concern over all these petty rates and their measurement becomes elevated to usurp the true scope and grandeur of the subject.

The true and substantial well-being of a people is called *economic freedom,* and the scope, the purpose, of economics is to provide for the practical possibility of all to live in economic freedom and thereby have the opportunity to develop fully the innate potential of being intelligent, creative individuals. For this to be experienced in daily life requires that the rule of justice prevails. The liberating and dignifying effect upon human life of the rule of justice constitutes the essence of this book.

CHAPTER 1

What is Economics *For*?:
the function of economics

The purpose of economics is to lift people's lives, to allow them to live a fuller and more complete existence as human beings; to enhance and enrich human life.

LEON MACLAREN

The purpose of aeronautical engineering is to inform the building of aircraft that are safe and efficient. The purpose of medicine is to keep the human body healthy and functioning in a manner fit to serve its purpose. The purpose of history is to provide lessons for the future, and inspiration and courage from the study of the lives of great people. But what is the purpose of economics? A journalist asked recently, "Why is there economics instead of nothing? What good is economics?" The frustrated journalist noted that economics must be good for something, but that it is not clear what this "something" is; and that mainstream economists seem to be unaware of any problem, and thus are incapable of advocating for their science. Intelligent lay people must be tempted to align with the frustrated journalist and think that economics might be good for nothing.

If aircraft constantly crashed, it would not be said that engineering is good for nothing but rather that it had gone astray in the application of sound principles in the building of the craft. When human bodies fail to be healthy it is not said that medicine has failed but rather that wrong principles, or no principles, of nutrition have been applied. Similarly in the case of economics. Economics itself has not failed. It *does* have a function and there is good and useful economic knowledge available – *very* good knowledge and very useful knowledge. However, in the face of the pressing economic problems that confront the world, in many different places and on many different fronts – from rioting, dispossessed youth to hungry, starving millions – it is obvious that the wrong knowledge, or no knowledge, has been applied. Economics as it is commonly professed simply does not seem to know the answer to the vexing socio-economic problems of our times. And so intelligent lay observers are tempted to conclude that mainstream economists are incapable of solving these problems; and, indeed, that economics itself does not have a purpose. "Many feel completely lost. Only a few still dare to be critical and ask what the reasons are for the present threat to the lives of human beings and to nature, and whether there are any alternatives" (Ulrich Duchrow, in Mofid 2002, p. 1).

To say the very least, there are major shortcomings within the discipline of economics. And there appears to be a fixation in the minds of economists with discussing and presenting the subject in the manner they have become accustomed to – irrespective of, in fact in total disregard for, all its accompanying shortcomings. This situation may be likened to how James Wolfensohn (2010) described the running of the World Bank: "…you realise that the invisible internal structures – the hierarchies and networks and fiefdoms that had solidified over the years – are every bit as massive and immovable as the expensive new headquarters edifice" (pp. 261-262).

Economics has a purpose that seems to have been forgotten. Whilst it is generally well-understood that economics is to do with the production and distribution of goods and services, it seems to have been overlooked, or forgotten, by economists that this production and distribution is done by and *for* human beings. "It follows, then, that it is mankind who is principally to be considered in economics" (Young 1996, p. 1). Because it is a fundamental desire of the human being to be free, a consideration of freedom in the economic sphere is of first importance in the study of economics. However, because economic freedom[1] is now unheard of, economics is rudderless. It is without direction. It has degenerated into a mishmash, a proliferation of ideas, opinions and beliefs, commonly expressed mathematically by professors of economics in an attempt to create an impression of precision and intellectual rigour. The subject, and therefore its function, has become lost in the marketplace of technical jargon and pronouncements of academic specialists vastly over-trained in theory and seemingly incapable of exercising simple observation and commonsense. The talking points of economists revolve around inflation, the unemployment rate, the exchange rate, the balance of payments, structural deficits and the like, most of which talk confuses the lay person – the very person whom economics is meant to serve – and has caused a mass "turn-off" of interest in the subject. And what should be the most important, the most relevant talking point of all, which is the business of getting a living, is scarcely mentioned. "Getting a living is the most practically important of all questions because everyone must answer it before going on to explore and then express the possibilities of freedom" (Thoreau [1906] 1951, p. 164). "All these men (successful New York financiers) learned well the art of making money, but not one of them learned how to live" (Mofid 2002, p. 5). It has been said of neoclassical (contemporary) economists:

...They have emasculated the discipline, impoverished economic thought, muddled the minds of countless students, rationalised free-

---

[1] Chapter 9 provides a full discussion of economic freedom.

riding by landowners, taken dignity from labour, rationalised chronic unemployment, hobbled us with today's counterproductive tax tangle, marginalised the obvious alternative system of public finance, shattered our sense of community, subverted a rising economic democracy for the benefit of rent-takers, and led us into becoming an increasingly nasty and dangerously divided plutocracy (Gaffney and Harrison 1994, pp. 30-31, 224).

And Mofid (2002) says:

It is my firm belief that economics, and the way in which it has been taught at our universities worldwide, bears a major responsibility for the existence and persistence of these world economic crises. Modern economics has major shortcomings: it concentrates almost totally on self-interest motives and shows little respect for, or understanding of, the true human values of community, common good, morality, ethics and justice.

Further, the subject as a teaching discipline has become fragmented. A cursory glance at the University of Melbourne's Department of Economics reveals a bewildering number of subject offerings to students, including International Trade Policy, Money and Banking, The Economics of Taxation, Behavioural Economics, Time Series Analysis and Forecasting, Models for Insurance and Finance, Quantitative Methods, Environmental Economics, Environmental Economics and Strategy, Globalisation and the World Economy, Economic Development, Economics of Food – and the list goes on! The subject has been broken down into a myriad of "pieces", each piece having become the province of some highly trained "specialist", who, when questioned about any aspect of economics outside his or her narrow field of specialisation quickly replies, "That is not my area"! More and more is known about less and less. The result is loss of overview, loss of the importance of fundamentals, loss of perspective and, in particular, loss of direction for the subject in its wholeness. With its teachers representing a multitude of fragmented splinter groups, any vision of a grand and meaningful subject has vanished.

Similarly with respect to research, economics has become marginalised. This may be demonstrated easily by noting the titles of articles in prominent academic economics journals. In one of these journals, *The Australian Economic Review*, the following are the titles of several of the articles published in issues from 2011–2012:

- *Developing the Statistical Longitudinal Census Dataset and Identifying Potential Uses*
- *Trade Marks and Performance in Services and Manufacturing Firms: Evidence of Schumpeterian Competition through Innovation*
- *Sterilised Interventions within a Heterogeneous Expectation Exchange Rate Model*
- *Neuroeconomics: Investigating the Neurobiology of Choice*
- *The TRIPS Agreement and an Experimental Use Exception for 'Research Tools'*

Research in economics is largely dealing with trivial, socially irrelevant issues, discussed only because they can be turned into material "suitable" for publication by academic economists and thereby secure for them a promotion.

And so, economics is in a mess. Rather than the discipline being looked to for solutions to real economic problems, it is more likely to be the butt of jokes.

Economics, over the years, has become more and more abstract and divorced from events in the real world. Economists, by and large, do not study the workings of the actual economic system. They theorise about it … If economists wished to study the horse, they wouldn't go and look at horses. They'd sit in their studies and say to themselves, "What would I do if I were a horse?" (de Soto 2000, p. 14, quoting Ronald Coase, *The Task of the Society*).

What has gone wrong? Alarmed at what he saw as a malaise in community thinking, Barry Jones warned, quite a while ago now – 1982 in fact – Sleepers Wake! In its current degenerate state, economics is a hindrance to human development and the cause of endless frustrations.

But it hasn't always been this way. In its proper form economics has the capacity to serve and assist human development. In 1879 Henry George (1992, pp. 559-560) said the following of economics (*Political Economy* as it was then known): "...A social state is possible in which poverty would be unknown, and all the better qualities and higher powers of human nature would have opportunity for full development".

Economics, properly considered, begins with the practical question of getting a living. It does not end there: indeed its full and proper function is to inform leaders and lawmakers such that the regulation of everyday economic affairs will assist and encourage a refinement of behaviour and the rise of the best of the human qualities. But it begins with the question of getting a living. Plato said, "The whole point of our legislation was to allow the citizens to live supremely happy lives in the greatest possible mutual friendship" (*Laws* 743).

Economics is meant to be a servant of mankind. It has a grand function to perform, and is, therefore, a grand subject. "The purpose of economics is to lift people's lives, to allow them to live a fuller and more complete existence as human beings; to enhance and enrich human life" (MacLaren 1943, p. 276). Economics is about wealth. It is about abundance. This world is a richly abundant place, generously endowed with resources of all kinds. The application of human labour and intelligence to and upon these resources has the outcome of goods and services, and the limit to this output is only one of the availability and intelligence of human labour and access to natural resources. The possibilities here are very great: seven billion people and 50 million square miles of surface land area, plus the great resources of the oceans! Indeed, currently there is sufficient food produced in the world for every one of its seven billion human inhabitants to have a daily intake of 3,500 calories.[2] Economics, properly considered, is the science of prosperity: prosperity in terms of both material wealth and human spirit.

Economics and law

Any rational consideration of the true and substantial happiness of people needs to take account of the obvious fact that the human being is gregarious by nature. People naturally want to live in communities rather than in isolation. "Man is social in his nature. He does not require to be caught and tamed in order to induce him to live with his fellows" (George 1879, p. 509). Now community life requires rules or laws. With respect to economics, laws are required because in a community certain things have to be shared. For an individual living in physical isolation the question of sharing does not arise. But in a community of people certain resources have to be either shared or allocated for specific individual – "private" – use. The very essence of economic law is the terms upon which common resources are shared and upon which private resources are owned. The question of how this allocation of resources is managed is a very important one because at its core is justice, and the rule of justice is central to human development.[3] It is, therefore, central to economics.

Prosperity is natural, poverty is unnatural

The human being is born with, and lives with, desires. He or she desires and needs a range of goods and services in order to "keep body and soul together". Further, fundamental to economic life is human labour or "work", which provides these goods and services. Hence, in the very existence of every man and woman is a beneficent coincidence: the

---

[2] Steven Mosher, President of the US Population Research Institute, in *News Weekly,* 31 March 2012, p. 13. Mosher wryly notes: … and you wouldn't like how you looked at the end of the year if you consumed 3,500 calories a day!

[3] A full discussion of justice follows in chapter 6.

existence of needs and desires on the one hand, and the capability of work on the other. The one – the latter – takes care of the other. And this coincidence is not only beneficial, it is natural. The upshot of this coincidence is that poverty and deprivation are not natural. They are not naturally occurring phenomena. In a state of natural freedom, the appearance of poverty for a people would be accompanied by an immediate engagement in work, the fruits of which would dispel the poverty.

Except for the taking of vows and the like, no one voluntarily accepts poverty. Poverty is a state of existence imposed upon people. It is a state that they have to, but do not voluntarily, accept. Given that mankind is naturally equipped to meet his or her needs, poverty must involve some factor that is not in the natural set-up. The extreme end of the scale of poverty is physical starvation, and no able-bodied human being will lie around waiting for starvation "to happen". He or she will naturally, and vigorously, "do something about it", exactly in the same manner as a man who is being choked of air by another will fight with every ounce of his available strength to regain his freedom. A hungry man, much more so a starving man, will go to work to produce or find food. But he must be allowed to. He must have access to the opportunity to do so. Poverty exists and continues to exist because this opportunity is denied. He or she will continue to live in poverty only if prevented in some way or another from going to work to alleviate that wretched condition.[4] Poverty is not just a physical disaster. It is a psychological disaster. Poverty humiliates.

Plato discussed both poverty and income distribution. "Poverty is a matter of increased greed rather than diminished wealth ... Extreme poverty and wealth must not be allowed to arise in any section of the citizen-body, because both lead to both these disasters (civil war and civil disintegration)" (Makewell 2001, pp. 139-141).

Poverty and deprivation can be *alleviated* by way of gift. This, of course,

---

[4] Of course, poverty can limp along for a long time if those suffering its plight are placated by way of gift – gift of food and shelter.

is what unemployment and other such benefits aim to do. But it cannot be *eliminated* by way of gift. The just and definitive elimination of poverty is by working for what is needed but lacked. Gift is only a temporary help, and if living by way of gift becomes permanent, then the duty to work and provide for oneself and one's dependants is denied. Poverty cannot be eliminated by gift, need not be eliminated by gift, should not be eliminated by gift. Living by way of gift is demeaning to the human spirit. Living by way of gift defiles the dignity of labour.

The opportunity needed by starving human beings to relieve their plight is unconditional access to a work site. At the most basic level it means free and unhindered access to the natural resource, land; in terms of a city environment it means free and unhindered access to a work site appropriate to the given mode of work. Given this access, those concerned would immediately avail themselves of it and go to work to put an end to their plight. The fact that thousands of people starve to death every day is cruel testimony to the fact that they do *not* have access to land. Why they do not have access is the discussion of chapters 3 and 6. Sufficient to note, at this point, that extreme poverty is a state people are forced to accept, and that proper economics explains, precisely, the *mechanism* of enforcement. People live in poverty because either they are denied access to the natural resource that is capable of ending their sorrow – a worksite; or they are forced by landlords to pay a cripplingly high share of their production as rent. This is a major cause of poverty in third-world countries, but, unfortunately, most economists miss this point – because of a lack of understanding of the special nature of the resource, land.

Here, then, is another aspect of the function of economics: to see that the opportunity to work is made readily available to every able-bodied human being. Whilst economics is not solely about the alleviation of poverty, it would be both hypocritical and cruel if it could not explain the cause of and remedy for this ugly dis-ease.

Four foundation principles

What will be said throughout this book is grounded on four principles[5]. These principles are taken to be true by the author, not just for the sake of the argument herewith, but as true in themselves. They are:

1. There is such a thing as justice
2. Existence on earth is not entirely a physical matter; life has a spiritual or metaphysical aspect
3. Work is essential to the well-being of everyone
4. There is an important effect of work beyond the obvious one of providing for necessary goods and services.

First, there *is* such a thing as justice. Justice is not merely an idea, nor simply a wish nor the ideal of a dreamer. There is, now, right across the world, a very great departure from the rule of justice; but nonetheless, justice as a practical ideal does exist. It is not only an ideal – it is entirely possible, and desirable, that it be a living reality. Everybody knows about justice. A sense of justice is, in fact, understood by everybody, and this sense has become embodied in common sayings such as "a fair go". It is summed up in that wise utterance, "The labourer is worthy of his hire". Whilst justice is well understood in principle, it does not prevail commonly in practice. Greed is a perversion of justice; and concurrent with a rise in selfish actions *social* values and actions diminish. However, there *is* such a thing as justice, and its practical application would ensure that *all* and not just some benefit from prosperity. This is the test of justice – the absence of which is keenly felt!

Second, mankind's existence on earth is not entirely a physical matter. Life involves two distinct aspects – spirit and matter. All partake of both. The real and substantial purpose of life is to become a better man or woman for having lived, a happier man or woman for having lived.

---

[5] The four noted here will be further elaborated upon and expanded to a list of seven in chapter 3.

It is not to maximise some assumed physical "good" such as monetary wealth or leisure time. It is an observable fact that the continued acquisition of material wealth does not necessarily lead to happiness, and in fact commonly has little correlation with it. Happiness and well-being are not related to the accumulation of more and more *things*. True and lasting happiness is not to be found through the getting of more and more of the material universe. For full happiness the *whole* person – body, mind and spirit – needs fulfilment. The material universe certainly cannot satisfy the spirit, and a person poor in spirit can never be truly happy ("…When a man dwells on the objects of sense … he cannot expect peace and he cannot expect happiness" (*Gita*, chapter 2)). The author of a contemporary economics text says:

> An economic system, let me stress, cannot be reasonably judged just by its material achievements. Economic systems involve people in a web of social inter-relationships and different patterns of social relationship have different psychological repercussions. Though two different systems of economic organisation achieve the same material ends, depending upon how individuals relate one to another in a system, systems are likely to have different psychological impacts. Means are important in themselves. They themselves are factors in human happiness. We must consider not only the influence of a method of economic organisation on scarcity but whether it promotes a sense of belonging or alienation for individuals, encourages individual responsibility, development and creativity and allows reasonable variety in their tasks. Sociological and psychological elements of this kind may be no less important than economic ones in reaching our decisions about desirable forms of economic organisation … From an ethical point of view a society which is super-efficient may not really be efficient at all (Tisdell 1972).

In a similar vein Pope John Paul II said: "A temptation to be resisted is to subject technological development to the logic of profit, or non-stop economic expansion, with no care for the true good of humanity" (Kwitney 1997, pp. 362-363); and de Soto (2000, p. 2) notes:

> From Russia to Venezuela, the past half-decade has been a time of economic suffering, tumbling incomes, anxiety and resentment; of 'starving, rioting and looting' in the stinging words of Malaysian Prime Minister Mahathir Mohamad … For much of the world, the market-place extolled by the West has been supplanted by the cruelty of markets, wariness towards capitalism and dangers of instability.

And Dr Mahathir is not alone in speaking of "the cruelty of markets". "Materialistic values of wealth, status and image work against close interpersonal relationships and connection to others, two hallmarks of psychological health and high quality of life" (Kasser in Hamilton 2005, p. 14).

The third and fourth principles on which this book is founded – that work is essential to the well-being of everyone, and that there is an important effect of work beyond the obvious one of providing for necessary goods and services – will be discussed fully in chapter 5. What is noted at this point, though, is that life on earth is impossible without work; that it is a human *duty* to work; and, indeed, that it is *natural* to work. This is a very different view from that of the contemporary economist, whose view is that work is a *disutility* to the one who works, a nuisance, something to be tolerated, and that the only reason anyone works is that they are paid to. Work is *not* a disutility, it is not a nuisance, it is not something just to be tolerated. Thinking that it is a disutility, a nuisance, something to be tolerated, is false thinking, based on a complete misunderstanding of the fundamental nature of mankind. Viewed rightly, human work is a function of the highest value and importance.

Economics is the science of justice – of the conditions necessary for justice to rule. It is a noble subject with lofty ideals and values. If it were not so it would be of limited use to the noble creature, man. The spectrum of economics begins with a recognition of the need for the basic physical conditions of life on earth and ends with a consideration of the divine. Such is the scope of truthful economics. So important to economics is an adherence to a moral foundation of social and cultural life that Chief Rabbi Lord Sacks (2011, p. 11) said, and David Landes (1999) supports him:

> If Europe loses the Judeo-Christian heritage that gave it its historic identity and its greatest achievements in …economics, it will lose its identity and its greatness, not immediately, but before this century reaches its end. … The Christian moral foundation of social and cultural life was what made possible the emergence of capitalism.

The sentiments expressed by Henry George, Henry David Thoreau, Leon MacLaren, John Paul II, Clem Tisdell and others outline the "mind-set" with which proper economics is to be approached, a mind-set permeated by benevolence, grace, propriety, generosity, humanity, kindness, and justice. The well-known mainstream economist, John Maynard Keynes, would agree when he said: "Economists are the guardians of the possibility of civilisation".

CHAPTER 2

Where It All Began

This disposition to admire, and almost to worship, the rich and the powerful, and to despise, or, at least, to neglect persons of poor and mean condition, is the great and most universal cause of the corruption of our moral sentiments. ...Respect and admiration are due only to wisdom and virtue.

ADAM SMITH

Of all the names familiar to students of economics, that of Adam Smith comes first. Although Meek (1962) suggests that the French *Physiocrats* were responsible for the birth of economics in the broad general form in which it has come down to us today, Smith is generally recognised as being the pioneer of the discipline and the first in the English-speaking world to address, in a systematic way, matters of economics. He is credited with being the "father" of economics as a formal discipline. The Physiocrats were at the height of their influence in the 1760s and 70s, just prior to the appearance of Adam Smith's major work. Smith was aware of their work, and was approving of it. However, the influence of the Physiocrats – which was strong at the time – waned quickly, and had effectively disappeared by the time Smith wrote. It is worthy of note, though, that the Physiocrats attempted a synthesis of economics, politics, and philosophy, in an effort to embrace all the influences impinging upon economic life. Given Smith's high standing amongst contemporary economists, it would be useful to look at what he said, writing in the eighteenth century.

Adam Smith's most famous work is *An Enquiry into the Wealth of Nations,* popularly known as *The Wealth of Nations,* and it was published in 1776. The Wealth of Nations has been described as "the effective birth of economics as a separate discipline". It became the foundation stone upon which the discipline has been built. It represented a "first" in its time for a systematic examination of what we now call "economics" but which was then called "political economy". Smith engaged in a very wide-ranging, sometimes rambling discussion of the subject. However, economists are keen to single out that part of his dialogue where he referred to the existence and operation of an "invisible hand" – a discussion by Smith about how economic transactions between individuals take place smoothly and "as if by themselves", empowered and guided only by the self-interest of the transacting parties. Smith believed that the effect and power of self-interest meant that there was no need of any control or direction from "outside"; hence his terminology, the "invisible hand", which hand guided the smooth functioning of economic transactions.

However, contemporary economists do not speak much of the "invisible hand". Rather, it is now referred to as "the market", or "market forces". Of course, there are two primary market forces at work: supply and demand. Smith attributed the smooth interaction between these two as being due to the workings of an invisible hand, whereas today this smooth interaction is referred to as the self-motivated operation of market forces, with profit being the motivator. Hence we now have terminology including "the free market", "market capitalism", a "market economy", all of which terms mean the same thing as Smith meant when he spoke of economic transactions being guided by an invisible hand. The upshot of all this is that proponents of free, unregulated markets quote Smith as their "authority" for the advancement of free market economics. It will be suggested, shortly, that Smith would be horrified to see the extent to which his "explanation" of the operation of the forces of supply and demand and the invisible hand has been taken by contemporary economists as justification of and authority for a policy of complete deregulation of financial and commodity markets – policy adopted by Australia today, to the great detriment of many of her population.

A second familiar section of *The Wealth of Nations* is the discourse on what is now described as the "specialisation of labour", which Smith illustrated by his description of the manufacture of pins. There is a detailed discussion of the different parts of a pin and the manufacture of each of these "separate" parts by different individuals, leading to a great efficiency in the production of pins. Having a number of pin producers working together, each specialising in fashioning a part of the pin, leads to the production of a far greater number of completed pins per time period than if each of the pin workers separately produced the whole pin. This process – the specialisation of labour – is well known and practised widely today. While Smith discussed other economic issues at length, including taxation, he pioneered dialogue on these two fronts: the workings of what is now referred to as "the market", and the specialisation of labour.

A very great deal has been made of these two concepts since Smith's time. However, it is highly unlikely that he would agree with twentieth- and twenty-first-century interpretations of and commentaries upon his work. First, he would be horrified to hear of the adoration and veneration bestowed upon "the market" by today's economists (and almost everyone else in the western world). He would be horrified to see the extent to which his dialogue on the workings of the invisible hand has been the source of justification for a wholesale handing over of economic activity to the unfettered operation of market forces – to the "free market". Obvious examples of this include the sale – privatisation – of our public utilities and health service providers, which, for centuries, had been run on the principle of service, not profit. Because of Smith's constant emphasis upon human well-being – obvious from his writings that include discourses of the following ilk: "...to feel much for others and little for oneself, to restrain our selfish and to indulge our benevolent affections, constitutes the perfection of human nature" – it may be concluded that he was interested in directing self-interest to the common good. Lord Sacks certainly believes so; and sees today's emphasis upon the supremacy of "the market" as becoming:

> ... a means of empowering self-interest to the *detriment* of the common good. Instead of the market being framed by moral principles, it comes to *substitute* for moral principle. If you can buy it, negotiate it, earn it and afford it, then you are entitled to it – as the advertisers say – because you're worth it. The market ceases to be merely a system and becomes an ideology in its own right (Sacks 2011, p. 13).

Second, Smith would be astonished and dismayed to witness the extent to which the specialisation of labour has been carried in the modern factory – where a commonplace, mind-dulling occurrence is human beings on a product assembly line being given the sole daily task of tightening a single bolt! The debilitating effects on human intelligence of the extremes to which the specialisation of labour has been carried, and the extremes in wealth concentration consequent upon the unfettered, unrestrained operation of "the market", clearly are not what he would have had in mind when he wrote *The Wealth of Nations*.

Unlike their widespread awareness of *The Wealth of Nations,* contemporary economists seem to be unaware that that was not Adam Smith's first book. That was *The Theory of Moral Sentiments,* published in 1759, during his tenure of the Chair of Moral Philosophy at the University of Glasgow, where he had been Professor of Moral Philosophy since 1752. Being unaware of *The Theory of Moral Sentiments* and its content renders any student of economics unaware of the full thinking of Adam Smith – unaware of the "whole man". It is plain from even a cursory reading of *The Theory of Moral Sentiments* that – as has been mentioned already – Smith's primary interest was the well-being of people, not the promotion of greed and selfishness. He keenly observed and studied human behaviour, particularly with respect to matters economic. Obviously, he was interested in human development. He wrote at length about behaviour that would move life in the direction of "perfection". He was interested in fostering generosity, humanity, kindness, compassion, mutual friendship and esteem, not a rampant push for profit nor a drifting into dullness of mind and poverty. The following quotations from his 1759 work make this plain:

> And hence it is, that to feel much for others and little for ourselves, that to restrain our selfish and indulge our benevolent affections, constitutes the perfection of human nature; and can alone produce among mankind that harmony of sentiments and passions in which consists their whole grace and propriety ...
>
> There is another set of passions, which a redoubled sympathy renders almost always peculiarly agreeable and becoming. Generosity, humanity, kindness, compassion, mutual friendship and esteem ... please the indifferent spectator upon almost every occasion.

Plato says similarly. "The whole point of our legislation was to allow the citizens to live supremely happy lives in the greatest possible mutual friendship" (*Laws* 743 (in Makewell 2001, p. 140)).

Both Smith and Plato were well aware of the human propensity to venerate riches, and simultaneously to neglect or even "look down on" the poor. Overt admiration of the rich is commonplace – see, for example, the regular and pompous publication of *BRW's* list of wealthiest people. Of this propensity Smith said:

> This disposition to admire, and almost to worship, the rich and the powerful, and to despise, or, at least, to neglect persons of poor and mean condition, is the great and most universal cause of the

corruption of our moral sentiments. ... Respect and admiration are due only to wisdom and virtue.

Plainly Smith was interested in promoting "*another* set of passions" – a passion for human dignity and refinement rather than the accumulation of physical wealth and regard for personal aggrandisement.

In light of the magnanimous minds whose influence shaped the early development of economics, there is a surprising dearth of reference to *morality* in modern-day economics. Indeed, economics is not commonly thought of as being connected with morality. "We no longer give much thought to moral progress – a prime concern of earlier times – except to assume that it goes hand-in-hand with the material" (Wright 2004, p. 4). To many observers economics is considered to be lacking in a consideration of morals, at best, and, at worst, to be amoral. This dearth of morality is surprising because this has not always been the perception of economics. The tendency to think of economics as being amoral is a relatively recent phenomenon. Clearly, Smith did not think this. Smith saw ethics, morality and economics as being interwoven, intimately connected. It is indeed surprising, then, that economics has shifted so far away from the view of its founder with respect to consideration for ethics and morality.

The dearth of morality in economics is not only surprising, it is troublesome. It is troublesome because economics impinges upon everyone. None escapes its effects. Few academic disciplines can claim that their subject matter affects everyone, directly, in the manner economics does. Economics is concerned with the material means of living and the conditions under which people work to earn the means of living, hence it impinges upon everyone. Pope John Paul II is on record (Kwitney 1997, pp. 337, 362-363) as being concerned about the need for economics to take account of ethical and moral considerations:

Market forces are never natural, but always constructed by people. They could play their beneficial role only when they functioned under individuals who are free, equal, and linked by solidarity, and under moral norms that are binding upon everyone … Science will destroy culture unless three temptations are avoided. The first is the temptation to pursue technological development for its own sake as if one should always do what is technically possible. The second temptation is to subject technological development to the logic of profit, or non-stop economic expansion, with no care for the true good of humanity. Third is the temptation to subject technological development to the pursuit of power, as when it is used for military purposes, and whenever people are manipulated so that they may be dominated.

However, you cannot *legislate* for people to be moral. You cannot legislate that people be honest. You can only legislate for penalties that will induce or encourage moral behaviour.

In a lecture to the School of Economic Science in London in 2001, Joseph Hyde (2001) brought ethics and morality in economics clearly to the fore. He said:

… In the subject economics, as based simply and purely upon the pursuit of self-interest, we have a denial of the true nature of civil society, and this has, as a consequence, led to the corruption of Political Economy as a subject. Instead of being the greatest of the social sciences, its blindness to the true principles of civil life has turned it into the servant of wealth and power, and the apologist for the gross injustice and suffering which we all know rules throughout the world. … We should not be surprised, therefore, if benevolence and goodwill, generosity and free gifts, which form the basis of our private, personal relations, have no place in our public and economic life, where experience tells us that quite different motives are usually at work.

Hyde's observation that "free gifts" form the basis of personal relations is both insightful and important. From it follows the question as to why free gifts are traditionally thought to be outside the scope of economics. In other words, why is economic activity thought to depend *solely* upon the profit motive? Whilst it is not being suggested that "free gifts" is the basis on which an economy could or should operate, why is there such blind acceptance of the free-market mentality which has self-interest as the sole motivator of economic activity and to which "free gifts" are unthinkable?

In 1982, Barry Jones warned of the real possibility of a coming period of "alienation and unprecedented social crises" (1982, p. ii). If the current health of our economy is measured by the commonly accepted standards of the official rate of unemployment, the rate of economic growth and the rate of inflation, then Barry Jones's predictions may be said to have been exaggerated, perhaps wrong. But if a wider, less technical, socially oriented view is taken, what Jones predicted may be seen to have actually happened. Gaffney (1994, p. 137) sketches the current socio-economic landscape as embodying "a worsening condition of labour, lower returns to saving, rising class divisions and social problems, and a fall of national stature".

Given this unhealthy – amoral – situation, and given that we probably now have more professionally-trained economists at work than in any prior era, the question should be asked, What has gone wrong? In particular, what has gone wrong with regard to the place of morality in the discipline of economics? People are not without sense of the importance and value of morality and ethics in their private lives, particularly family life. Why, then, have morality and ethics dropped out of view in economics?

Generosity, humanity, kindness, compassion, mutual friendship and esteem: this is where economics began. But these essential human qualities have now been given a price of zero. That is to say, they do not "count", they are not taken into account in any typical benefit-cost analysis of economic activity. Hence, one commentator has described modern economics as being *untouched by the breath of God, unrestrained by human conscience*. Contemporary economics has removed from its domain almost any evaluation at all of the essential human qualities, such as compassion, truthfulness, loyalty, trust, companionship, sense of community. This means that the cost of the *absence* of these qualities is ignored. These intangibles may be difficult to "price", given that there is no market for them and so they do not fit easily into the "market-based" thinking of economists. But that is no real reason for their being ignored. Their importance is revealed by their absence, and this absence has a *cost* – an obvious cost. This cost *can* be measured, at least partly. It is revealed in the cost of tax avoidance and the cost of corporate crime; and in the cost of human unhappiness, restlessness, greed and all the rest that arises as a result of ignoring these better human qualities. Again, in the terminology of contemporary economics, the price of these "intangibles" (compassion, truthfulness, loyalty, trust) is at least equal to the cost of the malevolent actions that their absence leads to.

Henry George, in 1879 (1992, pp. 559-560), said of economics ("political economy" as it was then known):

Political economy has been called the dismal science, and as currently taught, is hopeless and despairing. But this is solely because she has been degraded and shackled; her truths dislocated; her harmonies ignored; the words she would utter gagged in her mouth, and her protests against wrongs turned into an endorsement of injustice ... Freed in her own proper symmetry, Political Economy is radiant with hope ... Properly understood, the laws which govern the production and distribution of wealth show that the want and injustice of the present social system are not necessary; but that on the contrary a social state is possible in which poverty would be unknown, and all the better qualities and higher powers of human nature would have opportunity for full development.

From the lofty position of its start, how great has been the fall of contemporary economics! But there is a way up. The high ground has been made plain a long time ago.

CHAPTER 3

First Principles

Nothing is required and nothing will avail, except a little, a very little, clear thinking.

JOHN MAYNARD KEYNES

There are two aspects to life in a community: civil and economic. Civil life, in the greater part of the western world, at least, is protected by civil law, which protection allows its citizens to live in civil freedom. This is not the case in economic life, where first principles have been neglected or ignored altogether, and people do *not* live in economic freedom.

John Maynard Keynes held that "nothing is required and nothing will avail, except a little, a very little, clear thinking", and so he would roundly support, indeed urge, a return to first-principles in order to sort out the mess that economics is now in. The following is a summary of the seven first-principles in the study of economics that will be presented and discussed in the chapters to follow.

1. At the very root of an understanding of economics is an appreciation of:
   (i) the natural occurrence of the requirements for the production of wealth

(ii) site advantage, and

(iii) justice in the distribution of wealth.

2. There *is* such a thing as *justice*. Plato defines justice as being when wisdom or the opinion of the *best* is the guiding principle for action. The fundamental basis of justice is that "the labourer is worthy of his hire". Justice in the distribution of wealth may be stated in a single sentence: the full product of the marginal site belongs to the individual who worked on that site and the excess production on other, better-endowed sites, belongs to the community.

3. Existence on earth is not entirely a physical matter; life has a spiritual or metaphysical aspect.

4. Work is essential to the well-being of everyone. There is an important effect of work beyond the obvious one of providing for necessary goods and services.

5. Any solution to economic ills, particularly that of injustice in the distribution of wealth, lies in removing altogether the opportunity, indeed the possibility, of land being an investment good. Good and just economic law removes the possibility of gain without contribution.

6. The true banker's function is the establishment of creditworthiness. Interest has no place in real credit. The charging of interest is the consequence of not understanding credit and not understanding the real nature of money.

7. The essence of economic freedom is *independence*. Economic independence is the opportunity of being able to work and earn a living *without first having to come to terms with another party*.

With respect to the first of these seven principles[6] and its three aspects:

---

[6] The remaining six will be discussed in the chapters to follow.

(i) Human needs and wants, the desire to work, and the supply of raw materials and resources, are all natural

(ii) Work, by necessity, involves a site of land, and all work sites are not equally productive – some sites lend a productive advantage compared with other sites

(iii) Justice is the requirement for the proper distribution of wealth

(i) Human needs, work, and raw materials

Mankind is born full of needs, wants and desires, but coincidentally with two hands and a mind capable of being put to use to satisfy these needs, wants and desires. Further, man is born onto the surface of an earth teeming with raw materials and resources, the very things that are required for meeting human needs. The natural resources of the earth are present and available. The needs and desires of people are self-existent. Similarly with the ability and desire to work: it exists, it does not have to be created. Thus the stage is set for the individual to go to work to satisfy his or her desires. The only thing required of the economist in this regard is to remove any incentives not to work or blockages preventing work, such as inability to access natural resources.

It may sound trite and superficial to be drawing attention to these simple matters, but contemporary economics ignores them, firstly, and secondly, comes up with complicated analyses of economic situations which do not get any better for the existence of these analyses. In fact, the worst of them – world poverty, for example – seem to get worse. It is of first-importance that the simple, underlying principles of economic behaviour are stated, again and again if necessary, in order that the basis of pressing economic problems is understood and therefore able to be dealt with appropriately. To take just one example: when it is announced that a certain number of jobs have "been created", what has actually happened is that the people for whom a job is said to have been created are now allowed access to a work site, which access was previously denied them for one reason or another. This is the simple fact of the matter. It is not so much that a job has "been created" as that the natural desire to work in order to fulfil needs and desires has been allowed to express itself. Hindrances have been removed that previously prevented the people concerned from exercising their natural propensity to want to work. Or, to put the same thing differently, a work site has been opened up thereby allowing individuals to go to work. The natural desire to work is not "created". It already exists. Human beings are born equipped to work for the provision of their needs; the earth is a bounty of natural resources; and so the terrible human conditions of unemployment and poverty simply have no natural basis for their existence. Men and women *will* work to satisfy their needs, and so if these are not being met – and clearly they are not in the condition of poverty – then these simple facts are being ignored. And the solution is *not* in technically complicated analyses but rather in a restoration of first-principles.

(ii) Worksites and productive advantage

The production of anything at all is the outcome of human effort carried out upon a worksite – which, of necessity, involves the resource, land. The natural resources of the earth only require being worked upon in order to fashion them into a form suitable for human use. They do not require being created. Thus, two factors are involved in production: work and land. Work is obvious and universally appreciated. Land is obvious only in the case of agricultural production, and is not universally appreciated. In virtually all cases of production except agricultural production, the resource, land, is either ignored or taken for granted. Such is the importance of land to an understanding of economics that a separate chapter (chapter 4) is devoted to its discussion.

Land as a factor of production in cities is just as important as it is in the case of agriculture. However, land – that is, earth – is not obvious in cities because it is almost everywhere covered over with concrete or tar. Further, very little of it is required compared with the area of land required for agriculture. Hence, the economic importance of land in cities is generally missed, overlooked. But this does not alter its importance in the process of the production of goods and services. Because of the relatively small area of land required for work to take place in the vast majority of urban cases, land in a city is referred to as a "site".

Now application of the same work effort upon different sites will bring forth different results, depending upon where the site is. For example, a retail fashion shop will achieve much higher sales if located on a busy central shopping site than if it were located on the far edge of the city. In the case of agriculture, the very same inputs, intelligence and effort applied by a farmer to different paddocks (sites) will yield different results depending upon the natural fertility of the soil and the climatic conditions associated with the different sites. Thus, the first-principle applicable here is this: the same amount of effort and entrepreneurship applied to different sites yields different results. In other words, some sites have an *advantage* over others with respect to production.

The productive advantage of one site over another is called *economic rent* (or simply, *rent*) and is reflected in the higher price that a business is prepared to pay to gain access to the better site. In the commonly understood sense of the word "rent", it is the payment a business is prepared to make for occupancy of a better site. (Of course, it is also reflected in the freehold market price of the site). This much is well understood by any intelligent observer. However, what is not so well understood, and even where it is understood is ignored, is: What is the *cause* of the advantage of one site over another? and What are the *implications* of this cause?

Productive advantage of one site compared with another is due to the presence of factors that are entirely independent of the efforts of the occupant of the site. In the case of retail activity the major cause of advantage is the presence of a large flow of pedestrian traffic – that is, a large flow of potential customers. Another causal factor is the presence of efficient public transport. Now the important thing to note about this advantage of one site over another is that it is bestowed upon the site. It is not created by either the owner or the occupant of the site. It is *bestowed upon* the site by the presence and activity of the surrounding community. The advantage is "caused by" the community. The community, in the form of people, and government spending of those people's taxes on public infrastructure, gives some sites a productive advantage over others. In a large city this advantage of the best site over the marginal site is of enormous magnitude – the size of which is indicated by noting a fifty-storey high building erected on the best site compared with only a one- or two-storey building on the same-sized, but marginal site. The site upon which the fifty-storey high building is erected is twenty-five times more productive than the other site.[7]

The advantage of a particular site to its occupant is revealed by the amount of rent (lease) an occupant is prepared to pay for occupancy.[8] Now given that this advantage is created by the presence of the community and its infrastructure, the rental payment for the value of occupying the site should be paid to the community. "Earnings belong to the earner and location value in the midst of a community belongs to the community" (Stewart 2008, p. 101). The presence, the very existence, of the community is the cause of the productive advantage the site has, and so justice requires that payment for this advantage belongs to the community.[9] It is unjust that this payment be made to an individual, because he or she did not, cannot, create the value that is being paid for. Winston Churchill, speaking in the House of Commons in 1909, put the argument this way:

---

[7] Assuming equal value of production coming from the respective storeys of each of the two buildings. The marginal site is often (but not always) found on the edge, fringe, of a city.

[8] Strictly speaking, the advantage is revealed by that part of the rent payment that is attributable to the unimproved value of the site. It is the total rent payment minus that part attributable to improvements (including buildings) on the site.

[9] The argument here is about *site* value. Part of any normal "rent" payment made for occupancy of a property is usually for buildings and other man-made improvements to and upon that site, and this part of the payment is due to the individual who put the improvements there.

Roads are made, streets are made, services are improved, electric light turns night into day, water is brought from reservoirs a hundred miles off in the mountains – and all the while the landlord sits still. Every one of those improvements is effected by the labour and cost of other people and the taxpayers. To not one of those improvements does the land monopolist, as a land monopolist, contribute, and yet by every one of them the value of his land is enhanced. He renders no service to the community, he contributes nothing to the general welfare, he contributes nothing to the process from which his own enrichment is derived.

Community-created advantage (and naturally-occurring advantage, such as sea and hill-top views) is reflected in the price of the land concerned; and, unfortunately, "real estate is the bedrock of privilege" (Stewart 2008).

(iii) Justice in the distribution of wealth

Vital to truthful economics is that *justice* is required in the distribution of wealth (goods and services). There are two main contributors to the production of goods and services: the individual human being and the community in which he or she works. *Both* make their contribution. Only in the case of an individual living in total isolation and therefore total independence is the community not involved in production. This state of isolation is a rare situation; so rare in fact that it needs no consideration. Plainly, in any such cases as may exist, the question of justice is answered very simply. In a state of isolation there is nobody else, and so the entire production belongs to the individual. He alone produced it, it is his alone to enjoy.

However, this is not the common situation. The gregarious nature of the human being has him and her living in communities. Hence, when individual men and women work, they are working with the support and assistance of the community. This support and assistance takes several forms, the most important and obvious of which is that the community provides the buyers for the goods and services that are produced. This factor, usually overlooked entirely, is crucial to the success of *large* corporations, particularly. It is the community that constitutes the demand – "buying power" – for what is produced. Mass marketing is possible only because a community exists. Large-scale production, with its associated economies of scale, is possible only because a community exists. A second major support the community lends to production is the provision of infrastructure. Transport networks, power, water, law and order, are all commonly supplied by the community. And hence there are *two* contributors to wealth; and so justice requires that it be divided between its two contributors: the individual man or woman working on the factory floor and the community in which the factory exists. Determination of the precise valuation of each of the two contributions is discussed in chapter 6, *Justice*.

Specialisation of labour

The specialisation of labour is a major support to production. Not only does the community contribute directly to the productive effort through the provision of public infrastructure, its very existence allows for the *specialisation* of labour. Each person does not have to be his or her own cook, builder, mechanic, farmer. He or she can specialise – can concentrate their attention upon that line of work that is best suited to their natural abilities and propensities. Working in total isolation is a very uncommon, almost non-existent situation in today's world. Rarely does an individual work without in some way benefiting from the work and company of others. A non-economist puts it this way (McInerney 2006, pp. 115-116):

> … Talented, yes … They're artists … You can't have everyone in a family being an artist. And thank God for that. It would be an unworkable situation. Artists need support. They're helpless on their own … They

need gallery owners, framers, paint manufacturers. People to look at their work. Patrons…Musicians are the same, nothing on their own … They need constant reassurance. Audiences. People to make their instruments. Build stages. Sell tickets. It's the same with writers. They need readers, booksellers, publishers, printers …

Being able to concentrate the attention allows for an emerging stream of new ideas and inventions that flower in the minds of those who work with a love of, and full concentration upon, their chosen undertaking. The increase in production – wealth – coming from specialised work carried out within the support and environs of a vibrant, healthy, co-operative community compared with the output coming from the same work effort applied by the individual in isolation is very great. The volume of output and the complexity and quality of output may both be increased many fold due to specialisation, compared with the output resulting from one or just a few people working alone. Specialisation is a direct outcome of the existence of community.

The contribution of the community to productive output is immense. Its magnitude can be sensed by considering the sparse, meagre physical conditions under which the pioneers lived and worked in newly discovered countries in earlier centuries, compared with the communal wealth that surrounds people in the contemporary world. Pioneers had to work on their own, in isolation. There was little or no help or support available to them in the form of a community and its infrastructure. In stark contrast, the contribution of a refined, developed society toward facilitating and enhancing the productive efforts of the individual is large. It is crucial to recognise this with regard to the question of justice in the distribution of wealth. It is worth noting that the Roman consul, Cicero, is reported to have said that every man's wealth should correspond to his service to the community (Stewart 2008, p. 31).

If all land, everywhere, were entirely *homogeneous,* like seawater is homogeneous no matter where it is found; and if all people on the globe were spread evenly upon the face of the earth, the major reason for economics would not exist. But, of course, land is not homogeneous. In the case of agriculture, it is not of the same "quality" with respect to its key characteristics of location and fertility; and with regard to city life, people are gregarious by nature and so do not live spread evenly across the face of the earth. It is in these two phenomena – the differing nature of land across different sites and places, and the gregarious nature of people – where lies the fundamental reason for the need for economics. Homogeneous land and an even spread of people occupying the land would mean that no site of land would have any advantage over any other site, and the need for economics would not exist.[10] It would not exist because there would be no advantage of working on any one site compared with another, and so no site would be any more valuable than any other site, and there would not, then, be an allocation problem. There would be no question of allocation because any one site would be as good as any other.

And so these fundamentals, at the very root of any understanding of economics, are simple: the natural occurrence of the requirements for the production of wealth, site advantage, and justice in the distribution of wealth. The job of the economist is to inform policy-makers as to the "rules", or law, by which access to the naturally occurring resources needed for production is obtained, and under which production is distributed. Just as there are laws, including gravity, governing the physical world, there are laws governing social and economic behaviour. Some may not agree with this, and say that, except for the law of supply and demand (that is to say, the operation of the "free market"), there are no such laws. "My own belief is that there is a harmony between society and nature … and it is this harmony that we need to discover … The ideal, which is a home to reason, can become the practical" (Stewart 2008, p. 32).

---

[10] This is, of course, a most unrealistic assumption. For no one site to have an advantage over any other site would require not only that there be homogeneous land and an even spread of people occupying the land, but also that any public infrastructure was "evenly spread". Unrealistic, though, as the assumption is, its invocation allows for a significant point to be made.

Finally, it is important to note that the single economic aim of *increasing production* – that is, *economic growth,* which is widely prescribed by contemporary economists for the elimination of all manner of private and social economic ills – is not sufficient, because the question of justice remains. The pursuit of continually increasing production in the absence of justice in its distribution leads only to increasing concentrations of wealth, side-by-side with deepening poverty. "So we limp on, with large numbers trapped on the wrong side of globalisation, and nobody doing much about it" (Evans-Pritchard 2011, p. 19).

The purpose of good law is that justice may prevail, and for law to be good requires that there be proper knowledge in its formulation. This is the essence of economics: the knowledge to inform law-makers of the appropriate legal framework that will result in the rule of justice in the production and distribution of wealth – its distribution, particularly.

CHAPTER 4

The Special Nature of Land

God gave the land to the people, so why haven't they got it?

ANDREW MACLAREN, BRITISH MP 1922–1945

Why land is fundamentally different from the other factors of production

Of all the mistakes made by today's economists, perhaps the greatest is the failure to distinguish the special nature of the resource, land. Economics traditionally held that there are three factors of production: land, labour and capital; but most economists now consider land to be part of the factor, capital, and not different or special in any way. To contemporary economists the same "law" of supply and demand is assumed to apply to the natural resource, land, as it does to other factors. This single failure to understand the special nature of land is the cause of contemporary economics being unable to solve the pressing social problems of the day, particularly that of deep and deepening poverty existing side by side with great wealth and progress.

The special nature of land has long been recognised by all the great traditions. In the Bible, the book of *Leviticus* (chapter 25) speaks at length of the importance of land to the people, and prescribes a detailed system for its equitable distribution. The book of *Joshua* (2: 9) declares, " ... The Lord has given us this land", and, indeed, the early settlers of the Barossa Valley in South Australia took this very declaration as their motto when they began the work of settling that picturesque, fertile valley. These words – "The Lord has given us this land" – are inscribed on the memorial to the Barossa Valley settlers, which stands on Mengler's Hill overlooking the valley. In the ancient *Mahabharata,* in the Hindu tradition, is recorded: " ... Everything springeth from the earth and everything, when destroyed, mergeth into the Earth. The Earth is the stay and refuge of all creatures, and the Earth is eternal. He that hath the Earth, hath the entire universe with its mobile and immobile population" (vol. 2, p. 11).

Adam Smith, the recognised pioneer of the modern-day discipline of economics, spent a considerable amount of energy analysing the special nature of land in his *Wealth of Nations,* published in 1776; and a few years later, in the early part of the nineteenth century, the noted English economist, David Ricardo, spelt out in detail the phenomenon of land *rent* and its importance in the distribution of income. Around the same period as Adam Smith, a French group, the *Physiocrats,* developed an entire economic system based on the central place and importance of land. They believed (and rightly so) land to be the key factor in the workings of an economy. Indigenous Australians treated land as being "sacred", as did the American Indians, from whom we have the magnificent speech on land attributed to Chief Seattle, 1854:

> ... So we will consider your offer to buy our land, but it will not be easy. For this land is sacred to us ... Our dead never forget this beautiful earth, for it is the mother of the red man ... So if we sell you our land, love it as we have loved it ... And with all your strength, with all your mind, with all your heart, preserve it for your children (*The Web of Life,* pp. 4-5, 15).

And, of course, there is the great economist and philosopher, Henry George, who, in 1879 published *Progress and Poverty: an inquiry into the cause of industrial depressions and of increase of want with increase of wealth.* In this remarkable work George presents – reasonably, passionately, lucidly – the workings of natural law with respect to the special nature of land and its key importance in determining the distribution of wealth. "... To Henry George, man and life were meaningless without land; man was a very part of the earth and to take away from man all that belongs to man would leave him but a disembodied spirit" (George 1979, pp. 28-29). *Progress and Poverty* sold more copies in its day than any other book except the Bible.

The intelligent reader must be inclined to think that with this rich history of economic thought as to the importance of land, today's economists would be only too aware of this fact and take it into account, fully, in their policy proclamations. But not so! The rich legacy of knowledge of economic law that has been handed to us has been ignored! And the great natural resource, land, is attributed no more economic importance than the buildings built upon it or the creatures that move about on it.

One of the reasons for this failure to distinguish the special nature of land is its universal presence. Land is common-place. Hence, it is "taken for granted". A mind that always takes some phenomenon for granted generally will not understand that phenomenon, and hence will be ignorant of its true importance. The attitude of taking land for granted, of taking it to be just another factor of production, like steel or cloth or flour or wool, leads to serious error in the realm of economics. Land is special, and is so for the following reasons.

The reasons land is special

There are five distinct reasons land is different from the other factors of production; five distinct reasons it is special. **First, everyone needs it.** Human existence is impossible in the absence of access to land. The demand for land, or, to be more precise, the demand for access to land, is a universal and undeniable demand. Irrespective of the particular human activity in question, that activity can only be carried out if land is available. Access to a site of land is a necessary condition for any, and all, human activity, including, of course, that of simply living. It is necessary for purposes of conducting a business that there be access to land; it is necessary for flying an aeroplane or sailing a ship that there be access to land; it is necessary for establishing a home that there be access to land. Of course, the amount of land needed for the conduct of the multifarious human activities varies widely from activity to activity, but nonetheless, the need for land is universal.

Second, land is not a product. It is not produced. Its existence is not the outcome of human effort. All (man-made) production is the outcome of human effort. Land is not produced because it does not have to be produced. It exists. It is given. And it is given to the whole human race, to everybody. This is so, of course, because, as already noted, everybody (every body) needs it. And as is the case universally, what is needed in this great creation is provided by the omniscient Provider.

Now because land does not have to be produced it has no cost of production. *Improvements* made to and upon it *do* have a cost of production, but the land itself does not. Hence, any payment made for land is not made to cover the cost of production of that land. Land does not become land only when a purchaser of it parts with his dollars in payment thereof. This is a very different situation from that which prevails in the case of man-made goods. Payment for them is made to cover their costs of production, and hence to encourage them into existence. If no payment were made for man-made goods, production of them would cease. Land does not and cannot cease to exist; and it exists, in its entirety, irrespective of payments made for it or not.

Third, land has a market price only because people give it one. Again, this is in contrast with man-made goods, which have a market price that arises in the first instance from their costs of production. A site of land, then, that has an increasing market price over time is being *given* this increasing price – given it by those who want it. That price is entirely unrelated to any increase in the cost of production of that land (which, as already noted, was and is zero). However, it (the increasing price) *is* related to increasing levels of services provided to and around that land (such as roads and public utilities) and to increasing demand for that land. The fact that land has a market price only by virtue of being given one would have been an obvious fact to new arrivals in previously uninhabited countries. The first settlers simply found the land and then put it to use. They were certainly not hindered from using it because its price was too high! It had no price at all, and it had no price because there was no community to give it one when they arrived. It is only when a community is established that a price for land arises. The establishment of a community results in people wanting and needing access to land, hence a price for it arises.

These three reasons, namely: everybody needs it, it has zero cost of production, and its price is given to it by the population of people living on and around it, make land an entirely different factor from the other factors of production and entirely different from man-made goods. Failure to understand this difference renders *impossible* any proper understanding of economics; failure to understand this difference leads to all manner of administrative and political folly. One of the more insidious social aspects of this misunderstanding is the oft-repeated claim that "the cost of housing is going up" – to the extent that many of the not-so-well-off can no longer afford to buy a house to live in. This is nonsense – and is discussed in chapter 7.

The importance of land in the division of wealth

If air, like land, could be purchased and "fenced in" such that it was available only to those able and willing to purchase it at the asking price, then economic progress – economic growth – would be absorbed by the owners of air and would be reflected in a rising price of air. Those who "owned" the fenced-in, enclosed air would charge for access to it, and because of the unattractive nature of the alternative of going without air, human beings would pay as much as they could *afford* to pay for it. This would be the only limit to how much the owners could demand. Thus, its price would rise as the capacity to pay rose, and so the extent of the rise would be in step with the rate of economic growth.

But of the natural elements which are essential to mankind for survival, air can*not* be privately captured and made available only to those willing and able to purchase it. Only land can – air, fortunately, is too fine a substance to be "fenced in" and held – and so the owners of land, not air, absorb economic progress. Hence the steadily rising price of land that is so readily observable. Land (via rental payments asked of tenants or the market price paid by purchasers of freehold title) has a pivotal function in the determination of the distribution of wealth – in particular, in the determination of the *just* distribution of wealth. This function is spelled out in chapter 6, and is the ***fourth reason land is special.***

Hence, land is special not only because it has no cost of production, it is special also because it is the one natural – not man-made – factor of production the owners of which can ask their fellow mankind a price for its use. That is to say, it is the one natural factor of production that can be sold. Air cannot be *sold*. Sunlight cannot be sold. And the price asked for the use of land is based on only one criterion: the amount that people are prepared to pay. It is *not* based on cost of production – as is the case with man-made goods – because there is no production. Its price is simply the amount that people are prepared to pay for it.

Thus, land is not some quaint idea applicable to history of prior the industrial revolution. It is not stuff that was important only in the agrarian age. It is, of course, the basis of agriculture, but it is the same stuff that house are built on in the twenty-first century, it is the same stuff that is at the basis of our bustling cities of teeming millions of people, and it is the very thing on which *locational value* rests.

But there is more to the special nature of land than indicated by these four reasons, and that is to do with **security.** Because everybody needs land – nothing can happen without access to it, not even life itself – ownership of land leads to a sense of security. Contrarily, non-ownership engenders insecurity in those who are dispossessed. Naturally, a sense of insecurity fosters action toward alleviating that sense; in particular, action directed toward becoming a landowner. The desire to own land appears to be innate in the human being.[11] It is a strong desire, as may be seen from the so-called "dream" of people to own their own home; and, on a larger scale indeed, from the thoughts of the founding fathers of the United States who, following John Locke, believed that security of one's property was intimately related to one's freedom (Johnson 1997, p. 212). But perhaps the greatest example of this desire in recorded history is the concern for property ownership and security by the descendants of those who "knew what it felt like to be homeless for forty years as they wandered through the desert" (Sacks 2011).

Respected historian and described by some as "one of the greatest friends of sanity", Hilaire Belloc, described as follows the strength and ramifications of the instinct to own property:

> It has been found in practice, and the truth is witnessed to by the instincts in all of us, that widely distributed property as a condition of freedom is necessary to the normal satisfaction of human nature. In its absence general culture ultimately fails and so certainly does citizenship. The cells of the body politic are atrophied and the mass of men have not even, at last, an opinion of their own, but are moulded by the few who retain ownership of land and endowments and reserves. So property is essential to a full life … (Belloc [1936] 2002, pp. 27-28).

In Belloc's view, not only is property necessary to the satisfaction of human nature: its absence leads to the ultimate failure of culture!

---

[11] This is a relatively "healthy" desire. But experience shows that upon securing that amount of land (or securing anything else, for that matter) necessary for a comfortable life, the desire does not seem to end. It manifests as the desire for *more,* and so greed is born.

These, then, are the five reasons land is special. The first four reasons are matters of fact. The fifth, whilst not exactly a matter of "fact", appears to be the way humankind all around the world think and behave with regard to land.

The special nature of the resource, land, has been ignored by the great majority of mainstream economists and almost all social commentators, and it has been ignored for a very long time. The consequence of this act of ignorance is that there has been a grave loss of justice in economic affairs.

CHAPTER 5

The Special Nature of Work

A man should not be judged by the nature of his duties, but by the manner in which he does them. His manner of doing them and his power to do them are indeed the test of a man ... The man who works through freedom and love cares nothing for results. But the servant wants his pay.

SWAMI VIVEKANANDA

It is not uncommon to find contemporary economists referring to work as something to be minimised, a kind of curse – a "disutility" in the formal terminology – a negative kind of activity involving dissatisfaction, to be engaged in only in the event of being compensated (paid) for the in convenience and "pain" (disutility) necessarily incurred in working. Contemporary economics texts commonly contrast the "disutility" of work with the satisfaction or pleasure derived from leisure. Work and leisure are suggested as being opposites.

This view of work is a false view. Not only is it false, it is mischievous, a view that causes much trouble. It leads an individual to think that he or she should do *nothing* without being compensated for the effort; and so it leads to an attitude of *giving nothing* without receiving some "appropriate" compensation – an attitude of crass selfishness, of reluctance, of holding back.

Not only is this a false view of work, it is a view that is contradicted by the very behaviour of human beings. It is an observable fact that people love "doing things", love action, love "being involved", and some even say that they "love work". *This* view – of being willing and happy to be involved – is a view that is much nearer to the truth of human behaviour than the view that work is a "disutility". And this view is the reason Kahlil Gibran wrote in *The Prophet:* "Work is love made visible".

Work is essential to the well-being of everyone. Indeed, life on earth is impossible without work. It is a duty to work, a duty of the human being to provide for himself and his dependants. Work is required to make the resources of the earth suitable and available for human use. But to say that work is *essential,* that work is a duty, misconstrues its real nature: work is *natural.* People, quite naturally, want to work, and do not work only because they are paid to. Sheep do not grow wool because they are paid to. They grow wool because it is their natural function to do so. And so it is with the human being – to work is a natural human function. The reason for paying those who work is that one of the outcomes of work is production, and payment for work is the giving to the one who worked that which he or she produced. This is justice. Looked at aright, payment is the *outcome* of work, not its cause.

The intelligent design of this creation is such that, built into every human being is the *desire* to work. This desire may not always be recognised as the desire to work. Often people say that they like to *play* – play sport, play at gardening, play at their hobby. This "play" is just another name for work. It is work in a particular form, carried out or engaged in with a motive different from that behind the usual situation of wanting or need-ing to "go to work". Nonetheless, it is work – physical and mental exer-tion – and it is natural. It is a natural activity of human beings, and the fact that it is natural is easily observable. Nobody in normal health can remain entirely inactive for very long, even if given full and unconditional opportunity to do so. The desire to move, to "do something", is universal, and work is the putting into effect this desire. It is the manifestation of this desire.

The obvious and necessary benefit of work is the production of goods and services to meet human needs and desires, but behind and beyond this benefit is the effect of work upon the inner nature of the one who works. " ... If any work is done, good or bad, it must produce as a result a good or bad effect; no power can stay it, once the cause is present" (Vivekananda, p. 26). This effect will be either to refine, uplift and enlighten the person, or to make coarse, "narrow" and dark. Which of these two effects work has will depend primarily upon the motive with which it is engaged, also on the justice or otherwise in the conditions of the work environment, particularly the reward obtained.

A full discussion of the effect of work upon the inner nature of an individual is properly the province of philosophy, but with respect to the motive (with which work is engaged) it is plainly observable that human beings are, by nature, of widely differing dispositions. Human natures range from being "demon-like" to angelic. " ... This devil lives within us and gets out ... tipping the balance between cleverness and recklessness, between need and greed" (Wright 2004, p. 8). In addition to the basic function of providing necessary income, work presents the individual with the possibility of "cleaning up" and refining his or her inner disposition. "Demon-like" natures require work – and plenty of it – to remove their negative tendencies, to "make the demons honest". A disposition toward laziness will be remedied by having to "turn up", day after day, partake in and stick at regular work; a disposition toward dishonesty will be improved upon by complying with ordinary standards of honesty that prevail in a reasonable workplace; a disposition toward slothfulness will be improved upon by complying with quality control standards in a workplace. At the other end of the scale – for those men and women of already-refined nature and who are fit to accept the opportunity – engagement in work provides the opportunity to develop latent leadership skills, responsibility and creativity, and the opportunity for the practice and refinement of the higher human qualities of truthfulness, kindness, magnanimity and trust. Work provides a present opportunity for bad people wanting to be good people and for good people wanting to be better people. "That man who does his duty as he goes, putting his shoulder to the wheel, will see the light, and higher and higher duties will fall to his share" (Vivekananda, p. 26). And Plato, referring to work (in the form of "physical education") with respect to care of the soul, said: "… A man should not forget the real reason money was invented (I mean for the care of the soul and body, which without physical and cultural education respectively will never develop into anything worth mentioning)" (*Laws* 743).

The common view of work being "a necessary evil" and therefore an activity through which one should aim for the highest possible monetary reward, has lead to education – particularly higher education – placing an almost exclusive emphasis upon training people to *do* something, with little or no thought being given to the training and development of the kind, or quality, of person – the kind of person one wants to *be*. Fortunately, not everyone agrees with this common view.

> … We must prepare graduates for what they will *do* in life, but we also have a duty to help them to at least think about what kind of people they want to *be* … Experience, alone, cannot guarantee wisdom any more than reading books can. The lessons of life are only available to those who are ready to learn them … To prepare students to learn from experience, we need to go beyond vocational training. Life, death, tragedy, love, beauty, courage, loyalty – all of these are omitted from our modern vocational curricula and yet, **when it comes time to sum up our lives, they are the only things that ever really matter** … When asked about what kind of life they want to be living in five or ten years from now, students talked about **purpose, meaning, identity, integrity and relationships** … love and loss, memory and

desire, loyalty and duty, our world and our universe and what it means to be a human being (Schwartz 2011, pp. 12-13).

To help shed further light upon the real nature of work it is useful to consider unemployment. Unemployment is *costly,* very costly indeed. This cost is ordinarily measured by economists as being the cost of lost production and the direct payment of unemployment benefits. However, the most important cost of all is the negative effect unemployment has on the mental, emotional, and sometimes even the physical constitution of people concerned. It takes away their independence and the dignity associated with being independent, and renders them *dependent.* This is why "job creation, in Judaism, is the highest form of charity because it gives people the dignity of not depending on charity" (Lord Sacks 2011, p. 11). Dependency, on the other hand, has the propensity to turn people into being irresponsible, lazy, lacking in initiative, and weak. Of weakness, Vivekananda said:

> … Weakness leads to slavery. Weakness leads to all kinds of misery, physical and mental. Weakness is death … This is the great fact: strength is life, weakness is death. Strength is felicity, life eternal, immortal; weakness is constant strain and misery: weakness is death.

And of receiving something for nothing (unemployment "benefits" for example), he said: "The beggar is never happy. The beggar only gets a dole with pity and scorn behind it … He never really enjoys what he gets (Vivekananda 2009, p. 10). Bird (2011) confirms this. Speaking of the unemployed in Melbourne, and of Australia's annual Centrelink welfare bill of $85 billion, he said,

> … the jobless generation is a tragedy. Letting these young people waste away on the dole with no employment, no education or training, isn't just a tragedy for them. It's a tragedy for us all. We're looking at a generation of wasted youth unless something significant is done.

These young people will also go on to have kids, who will know nothing of their parents being employed.

Poverty – the close companion of unemployment – is "a kind of death, worse than fifty plagues ... Judaism has refused to romanticise poverty" (Sacks 2011, p. 12).

And so, work is not *only* about money. "Work is about more than money ... The highest reward for work is not what graduates get from it but what they *become* by it" (Ruskin 2011, p. 13). Work is giving.

> Give what you have to give; it will come back to you – but do not think of that now, it will come back multiplied a thousandfold – but the attention must not be on that. Yet have the power to give: give and there it ends. Learn that the whole of life is giving, that nature will force you to give. So give willingly ... And the more one struggles against this law, the more miserable one feels ... He (God) *allows* you to work. He allows you to exercise your muscles in this great gymnasium, not in order to help Him but that you may help yourself ... This is the proper attitude of work (Vivekananda 2009, p. 30).

In this current era of a high and increasing valuation being placed on "free" time, leisure time, "when everything that matters can be bought and sold, when commitments can be broken because they are no longer to our advantage, when shopping becomes salvation and advertising slogans our litany, when our worth is measured by how much we earn and spend" (Sacks 2011, p. 14), let not be forgotten the dignity of labour.

Economics is for the regulation of everyday affairs such that participation therein – work, in particular – will assist and encourage a refinement of human behaviour and the rise of the best of *the natural human qualities: magnanimity, generosity, uprightness, compassion, humility, trust.*

CHAPTER 6

Justice

Justice is the main pillar that upholds the whole edifice. If it is removed, the great fabric of human society must crumble into atoms.

ADAM SMITH, *Theory of Moral Sentiments*

Three billion people of the world live on less than $2 per day; 24,000 die every day from starvation; during May of 2011, some 46 million US citizens used "food stamps" (ABC 2011). What injustice! Obvious injustice!

These figures are alarming enough, but nothing could illustrate more graphically the absence of justice than the regular sight on our television screens of these tens of thousands of starving human beings; and the dreadful, frightening riots in the City of London (early August 2011). The situation of the starving is simply in-human; and some of the London rioters were described[12] as "disenfranchised youth" who have become sick of being disenfranchised and took the law into their own hands, robbing, looting and burning city buildings. And "as information and communications continue to improve and the poor become better informed of what they do not have, the bitterness is bound to grow ... At some point those

---

[12] *Herald Sun* (Melbourne), Wednesday 10 August 2011.

outside the bell jar will be mobilized against the status quo by people with political agendas that thrive on discontent. If we do not invent ways to make globalisation more inclusive … we have to face the prospect of a resurgence of the acute social confrontations of the past, magnified at the international level" (de Soto 2000, p. 225-226).

Economics exists to make possible the living together of people in communities in which all members may enjoy prosperity, well-being, harmony, and the opportunity to take and develop responsibility. It exists so that *all* people, not just some, may have these enjoyments and opportunities. For this to happen, justice must prevail.

The fundamental basis of justice is that "the labourer is worthy of his hire". Each is due to receive the product of his or her own efforts, and to receive it in full. This is justice, and justice fosters the dignity of labour. Adam Smith was plain about the importance of justice, and Ralph Waldo Emerson made the following pertinent utterance with respect to justice:

Always pay. For first or last, you must pay your entire debt. Persons and events may stand for a time between you and justice, but it is only a postponement. You must pay at last your own debt. If you are wise you will dread a prosperity which only loads you with more.

Plato defines "justice" as being when wisdom or the opinion of the best is the guiding principle for actions – actions of either individuals or the state. He relates justice to wisdom. "Injustice", he says, is when "fear and anger tyrannise over the soul". In *The Laws* (864), Plato says that injustice is the outcome of being dominated by one or more of the tyrants[13] and thereby losing one's freewill and volition. *Loss of freedom* is the injustice, which is essentially a condition of the inner person – although it will manifest in outer, physical circumstances and actions. Whilst the London rioters, for example, were accused at the time of being "gang members" – as distinct from sufferers of injustice – it was later reported (*Herald Sun,*

---

[13] Plato, in fact, identifies six tyrants: anger, fear, jealousy, desire, pleasure and pain.

August 2011) that the majority of people arrested in Britain's violent riots were not gang members, but young, poor and on benefits. It appears to be the case, then, that behind the actions of at least some of the rioters lay "fear and anger tyrannising over the soul", and so, according to Plato, injustice ruled. A sense of lack of well-being on the part of the poor and disadvantaged spilled over into riotous behaviour. Indeed Britain's Home Office and Ministry of Justice warned of the dangers of ignoring Britain's disaffected youth.

Everybody knows what justice is; everybody has a sense of justice. This sense, this knowledge, is instinctive. A strong sense of justice is revealed when anyone suffers an *injustice*. Injustice is keenly felt and known; and it is resented by those upon whom it is inflicted.

There a simple test for justice. In paying for a good or service, justice prevails when the payer pays willingly and with goodwill. Resentment by the payer signifies the presence of injustice. Similarly, with respect to the amount being paid *to* someone for the provision of a good or service – particularly the provision of labour – the provider must be fully satisfied with the amount received. Dissatisfaction with the amount having to be paid or with the amount being received results in resentment in the one who is dissatisfied, and so injustice is revealed by resentful consumers or resentful employees. Further, in a state of dissatisfaction, consumers and employees are likely to pursue the acquisition of wealth in the belief that that (wealth) will alleviate the absence of satisfaction. The result is that "desire will rule in the hearts and minds of people" (*Gita*, ch. 2); that is to say, people will simply continue to want more and more, thus perpetuating the state of dissatisfaction.

In chapters 1 and 5, particularly, was discussed the importance to the individual of *work* and the value of the output resulting from it. It is through and by work that the individual makes a contribution to the society in which he or she lives; and, of course, it is through and by work that the individual provides for his or her own material well-being. The discussion to follow will be concerned with justice in respect of wages or earnings rightly due to those who work. Economics is about people, economics is *for* people, and so it is only appropriate that a discussion on justice begins with a consideration of justice in respect of wages.

When people work, justice requires that each receives the full product of his or her labour. However, except an individual be working in total isolation, some part of the product of his or her work will be due to input from other human beings, because there will have been co-operation in its production in one form or another. This co-operation is an aspect of "community". Thus, and as has been discussed in chapter 3 above, there are two "agencies" contributing to production: the individual – through the application of effort, intelligence and skill; and "the community". Production is a team, or joint effort, it is not purely a "private" (individual) matter, and so the product cannot be said to belong entirely to the individual. Hence, justice requires that it be divided, with shares going to each contributor in accordance with the value of the contribution. Thus will be implemented the great saying, "Render unto Caesar (the individual) the things that are Caesar's and unto God (the community) the things that are God's". Precise measurement of the actual value attributable to each of these two sources will be considered shortly.

Most economists say that the *just* division of wealth is to be determined by "the market" – that is to say, that the division of wealth should be left to the market forces of supply and demand to decide, and that a free, unhindered market will deliver justice. Clearly, though, "the market" does *not* always deliver justice. The task, properly, of economics is to reveal to law-makers the determination of the value of the contribution of the individual and the value of the contribution of the community. The proper determination of these two values is essential if justice is to rule, and rule it must if society is to prosper. In Adam Smith's words:

Beneficence is less essential to the existence of society than justice. Society may subsist, though not in the most comfortable state, without beneficence; but the prevalence of injustice must utterly destroy it ... Justice is the main pillar that upholds the whole edifice. If it is removed, the great fabric of human society must crumble into atoms.

Earned and unearned income

Critical to the implementation of economic justice is an understanding of the concepts, *earned* and *unearned* income. An understanding of the difference between these two income streams is essential if justice is to be known in the economic realm. In essence, all economic activity is work upon natural resources, "land". By "work" is meant human exertion. That exertion may be in the form of physical labour or the application of intelligence, creativity and thought. The form that exertion takes does not matter; the point is that it is involved. So, central to production is human effort. Hence, because production depends upon human effort it rightfully belongs to him or her who made that effort. The production has been *earned;* it belongs to the one who worked to bring it forth.

Now it is possible – in fact, it is common practice – that the product of the effort of one individual is given to or taken by another. Unfortunately, this practice has become institutionalised, and is given the sanction of law. The most common form of it is the claim by landlords to "rent". A site of land is worked upon by an individual who exerts himself or herself – often in the form of not only being physically present at the site but working hard and long upon it – and the result, of course, is production. The landlord, though, in exchange for granting occupancy of the site to the tenant but without exerting himself one iota in the productive activity going on at the site, extracts part of the value of this production as rent. This rent is *un*earned income to its claimant (the landlord). The value of the production from which it (the rent) is extracted was *earned* by the tenant. It (rent) is *un*earned by the landlord because he or she has contributed nothing toward the productive process that gave rise to it. Such appropriation of wealth is legalised theft. "Logic and morality are insistent reminders that no one should be permitted to make an unearned profit merely from acquiring possession of land, a natural resource which no man has created" (Day 1995, p. 17). Except for that part of rent that covers the landlord's investment in and maintenance of improvements, rent extracted by landlords is a major form of unearned income. The other major form of it is interest. Interest will be discussed in chapter 8, *Credit*.

One of the "natural failings" of the human being is to be greedy. Greed is the antithesis of justice, but in the absence of effective law to ensure the rule of justice, greed will rule. Mofid (2002) is strong on this point (he speaks not of the greed of the individual, but of corporations):

> … a handful of big corporations are ruling us, controlling our minds as well as our bodies. Globalisation for them means giving big business access to a global market, to produce as cheaply as possible, and to make huge profits for their shareholders, with no regard for the rest of us. In their greed they show no loyalty to place or citizens. They come and go as they please. What happens to a society or community as a result of their actions is of no interest to them (p. xiv).

In the economic realm, greed will manifest in the form of wanting to get as much as possible for as little effort as possible. This is why "unearned" income is so attractive. Wanting much is not the problem. The desire for prosperity is natural. It is wanting much *without commensurate contribution* (in the form of work) that is the problem. Good and just economic law removes the possibility of gain without contribution.

With respect to justice, a practical example of the significance of personal exertion or *contribution* is revealed in succession planning by farmers. When farmers seek legal advice in planning for their retirement and the consequent passing on of the farm assets to their children, lawyers use the term, *sweat equity*. The one (or more) child who has stayed on the farm and worked after having completed schooling is entitled to a greater share of the inheritance by virtue of the fact that he or she has *worked* ("sweated") on the property, and thereby made a physical contribution to its value. Children who have left home and gone to the city to work are entitled to less of the inheritance in view of the "sweat equity" notion – they have made a lesser contribution. In justice, therefore, they are entitled to less.

Making the distinction between earned and unearned income is vital in the search for economic justice, and therefore is fundamental to taxation policy. The essence of justice is that the individual receives, in full, what he or she has earned and receives nothing of what is not earned; and what is earned is the value of the contribution. The value of the contribution is at least the amount of the wage or salary paid by an employer to that individual, otherwise the employer would not pay that amount – would not employ the individual at that wage rate. Now to take away any of this wage or salary, by taxation or any other means, is unjust. Likewise, the value of the community towards production reveals itself in site value – the value of the site upon which production takes place. Hence, site value belongs to its cause – the community – and justice requires that it be paid to the community. For an *individual* to receive any of this is to be in receipt of unearned income. It arises as a result of the presence and activity of the community; that is to say, it is *earned* by the community, and hence it belongs to the community. This is why the site-value land tax is the foundation of economic justice. Site value is the community's just source of income in exactly the same way that the contribution of the individual to production is the just source of his or her income. Hence, it is the job of the true economist to inform and advise law-makers that justice requires the implementation of a site-value land tax. This is why Mirrlees (2011) says, "The economic case for a land value tax is simple and undeniable".

Hence, the fundamental principle of proper tax policy is that income earned by the individual belongs to the individual and justice requires that *none* of it be taxed away; whilst income earned by the community belongs to the community and *all* of it should be taxed away (appropriated to the public purse). (The benefit principle, then, is the appropriate taxation principle to apply, not ability-to-pay). Thus, with respect to taxation policy, the two commonplace practices of (i) individual income tax (particularly the taxing of higher-income earners at higher rates) and (ii) not taxing site rents (or taxing them only at some arbitrarily low rate) are both unjust.

The just division of wealth in practice

The fundamental question is: How, *in practice*, is the value of the shares between the two rightful claimants – the individual and the community – to be determined? In other words, is computation of the value of these two shares tangible and definite? The answer to this question is *yes*, and may be verified by considering what happens when a new country is opened up and settled by pioneers. When the first settler arrives and begins work, his entire output is his own. The question of any division of it does not arise because in the case of the first settler there is no one else with whom to divide the output. There is no one else who might have a legitimate (or any other) claim to any part of it. Hence his earnings (wages) are the total value of this output. This is justice: namely, that the first settler's level of earnings is the value of the entire output from his productive efforts. Wages are determined *directly* by productivity. Wages for the first settler *are* productivity.

However, in progressing from the first settler to today's situation of very many people working in an established, industrialised community, the output coming from the work of an individual is not entirely his or her own. In our "new country being opened up and settled", division takes place – needs to take place – between the two rightful claimants *only when communal needs* arise. When settlers two, three and so on arrive, there is soon need for "community" expenditure – a school to educate the settlers' children or a bridge across a creek to enhance ease of neigh-bourly contact. Who should pay for it? In deciding who should pay for the school or bridge there is now the opportunity, indeed the need, to consider the contribution of the community to the total production of our little economy.

Determination of the productive value of the individual

As has been discussed already and as is obvious anyhow, all production takes place on sites of land. What is also obvious is that the same effort and skill applied to different sites produces different results. For the same input, output will vary from site to site. Further, there is a site (or sites) upon which the application of this same effort and skill will yield an out-put which, if remaining entirely in the hands of the individual applying the effort, will be just enough to provide an acceptable living. This site is known as the "marginal" site.

The share of output that belongs to the individual working in a com-munity is the amount that would be produced by that individual if he or she applied the same skill, intelligence and effort upon the marginal site. The marginal site is the least productive site in use, but it is the site upon which, or from which, an individual may work and earn an acceptable living – provided that all of the output remains the property of that indi-vidual. If any is taken away – in the form of taxation or any other charge – then what is left will *not* be enough to constitute an acceptable living. This concept of the marginal site, and, indeed, its existence in practice, is of fundamental importance in the study of economics. It is also a simple and clear concept to envisage.

In our ("newly settled") economy – in fact in *any* economy – not all possible work sites will be in use, and that site which was not previously occupied (and was, therefore, available for use) will now be occupied by the latest arrival seeking a site to work upon. This site becomes the mar-ginal site. It is that site which, of all occupied sites, benefits *least* from the productive advantage bestowed by the presence of the community and its infrastructure.[14] Prior to the arrival of the newest settler it was a vacant site, a site that nobody wanted. The amount that an individual can produce on this site belongs entirely to him or her. To take away any of it is an unjust action. It is his or hers, by right, because (i) nobody else wanted that site and hence production upon it was zero, and (ii) of all work sites in the community, this is the one that benefits least from "community advantage". Hence, the full value of the product from that site belongs to the individual. Technically, this value is known as the full product of the marginal site. This value, this amount, sets the *natural level of earnings;* it *is* the natural level of earnings – the amount to be paid to the individual. It is the yardstick for determining the value of the contribution of the individual.

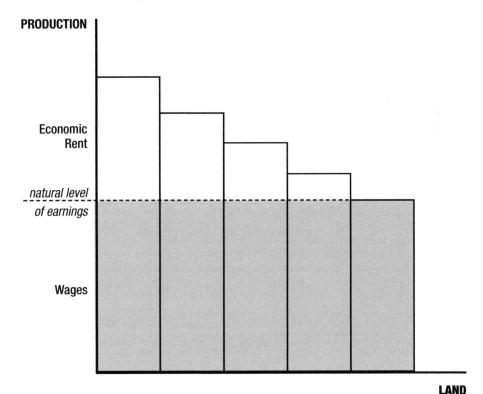

Figure 1: The two phenomena of economic rent and the natural level of earnings

---

[14] Discussed fully in chapter 3 above.

On sites more favourably endowed with community infrastructure (more favourably endowed than the marginal site) there will be an *additional* amount produced by the application of the same human skill, intelligence and effort. This additional amount is *economic rent*. Economic rent arises *not* as a consequence of any specific individual effort. It arises as a consequence of the presence of the community and its infrastructure, which, as already said, contributes greatly to the productive output. Figure 1 illustrates the two phenomena of economic rent and the natural level of earnings.

Economic rent – the value of the contribution of the community to the productive process – is the rightful source of income *for the community*. No individual, as an individual, can or does do anything whatsoever to produce or create it. This rent is the natural source of income for the community. It is natural because it arises as a consequence of the very existence of the community, and grows as a consequence of growth in community. When collected by the community it is the source of income for expenditure on the establishment and maintenance of community infrastructure: public utilities, law and order, public recreational facilities and the like. When, instead, it is privately appropriated it is capitalised to become what is known as the market price of land, and remains the property of the individual – unjust though that is. At the same time, the community is deprived of its natural source of income. Henry George ([1879] 1979, pp. 14-15) describes the injustice of private appropriation as follows:

> ... What more preposterous than that one tenant for one day of this rolling sphere should collect rent for it from his co-tenants, or sell to them for a price what was here (sites of land) ages before him and will be here ages after him ... This is the law of rent: as individuals come together in communities and society grows, integrating more and more its individual members, there arises, over and above the value which individuals can create for themselves, a value which is created

by the community as a whole, and which attaching to land, becomes tangible, definite and capable of computation and appropriation. As society grows so grows this value, which springs from and represents in tangible form what society as a whole contributes to production, as distinguished by what is contributed by individual exertion … Here is a fund belonging to society as a whole from which, without the degradation of alms, private or public, provision can be made for the weak, the helpless, the aged; from which provision can be made for the common wants of all as a matter of common right to each … By permitting individuals to appropriate this fund which nature plainly intended for the use of all, we throw the children's bread to the dogs of greed and lust; we produce a primary inequality which gives rise in every direction to other tendencies to inequality; and from this perversion of the good gifts of the Creator, from this ignoring and defying of His social laws, there arise in the very heart of civilisation those horrible and monstrous things that betoken social putrefaction.

According to Philip Day (1995), at the time of Australian federation the framers of the Australian Constitution were keenly aware of the need to prevent land speculation. Thus section 125 provides that the territory for the seat of government "shall be vested in and belong to the Commonwealth" (p. 73). The framers of the Constitution *knew* that if land rental values were permitted to be appropriated by private landowners then we would get the evil of land speculation. However, in spite of this foreknowledge of our ancestors, and of Henry George and his protestations, land speculation we have! "Well, that's exactly what's happening, albeit with the full backing of the law. It – the stealing by individuals or corporate groups of the rightful revenue of the community – is the economics of the madhouse, but the madhouse has been up and running for some time … Of course, some don't want it any different, for they're doing pretty well by playing the system. It's the way the mind-set is and few see past it" (Stewart 2008, p. 52); and " … The man of ability is an asset to society, and must render a service of value in return for the wealth he appropriates, whereas the man who owns land renders no service to the community in return for the wealth which he appropriates" (Hill 1999, p. 116).

Exaggerated emphasis upon the value of the contribution of the individual

Whilst the essence of justice is that an individual receives, in full, what he or she has earned, justice works "both ways": it is *injustice* for the individual to receive *more* than he or she has earned – that is, more than the value of his or her contribution.

It is plainly observable that in recent years and in certain areas of economic life there has been an increasing emphasis placed upon the perceived value of the individual. This emphasis may be seen in the escalation of monetary rewards accruing to certain individuals and groups of individuals. On the face of it a large monetary reward being given to an individual may be seen simply as a manifestation of good fortune; but there is a problem with large rewards – with unjustly large rewards – and that is in what this phenomenon leads to. Increasing levels of remuneration being paid to individuals only leads to claims for yet higher levels. Witness the explosive rise in the value of salary packages given to chief executive officers (CEOs) in recent years; and in the value of contracts awarded to top sporting personnel. In the interests of justice this phenomenon requires examination. Are these large monetary incomes *just*? Are they *fair*? Do they reflect the value of the individual contribution?

In answer to these questions it needs to be noted that the availability to the community of the superior management capabilities of an effective CEO, or the sporting prowess of a first-class athlete, does not depend upon the level of financial reward being paid the CEO or the athlete. These respective abilities and skills are "gifts"; they are innate attributes that the individuals concerned happen to possess. Certainly, the abilities and skills need to be refined and exercised, but their existence is not the product of monetary, or any other, reward, however great. They exist in the individuals concerned, they are not created by monetary reward. Of course there is the question of the *development* of these abilities and skills, and an argument might be put that this development would not happen in the absence of generous monetary reward being offered. But there is a world of difference between "generous" and "obscenely high". And further, there is much more to the story than just the individual possessors of these abilities.

The development of skills and abilities is, in no small way, dependent upon the existence of the community. Few, if any, individuals develop their innate abilities on their own, in isolation, without any input or influence at all from the surrounding community. An athlete needs running fields to train on. These are not the product of the individual athlete. An athlete needs coaches. These come from the community. An athlete needs fellow-competitors. These come from the community. An athlete benefits from the presence of spectators. These are of the community.

Further, it is the *duty* of the individual possessing such a talent to make it available. Sacks (2011), in fact, speaks of "responsibility … an obligation to use it for the benefit of the community as a whole" (p. 12). Certainly, a "fair" reward needs to be received for doing so, and a generous reward; but people, generally, are glad to make their talents available – they are made happy by doing so – and for the most part require only the opportunity to make them available, not a vastly superior monetary reward that is many times, often hundreds of times, the financial reward going to other skilled, contributing individuals. In almost any field that might be mentioned, the ground-breaking geniuses worked for minimal financial reward and, most importantly, this financial reward was not the stimulus for the supply of their talent. Mozart was forever in debt (he was *never* paid a lot of money for his superbly creative work), and Einstein did not accumulate any monetary fortune.

One of the plethora of unfortunate examples of greed that spoil economic life for many is the exorbitantly high salaries being paid some CEOs. The price mechanism in the market for CEOs and other top-level personnel in the various fields of endeavour acts as an allocating mechanism. Allocation of talent amongst competing employment opportunities is executed by way of price *relativities*. This situation is in accord with ethics and morality, as well as efficiency. However, the *absolute* level of remuneration concerned does not create the talent and expertise being spoken of; it does not bring it into existence. The talent, firstly, exists (as has just been said). It is latent (sometimes not-so-latent) in the individuals concerned. Second, it is developed, cultivated and refined through being used. It is developed through application. The fantastically high levels of monetary reward its possessors receive are not the cause of this valuable resource. If the salaries being paid the CEOs of the world's top 500 public companies were, for example, to be halved, there would not be a proportionate diminution in the supply of this resource. There would likely be *no* significant diminution. CEOs, then, are in receipt of high and substantial economic rents.

From a moral perspective this is a gross manifestation of greed; and greed is a perversion of justice. Further, there is an unfortunate flow-on effect of obscenely high salaries: they give rise to resentment and disillusionment on the part of the lower-paid members of company workforces, who witness salary differentials between themselves and those at "the top" of the order of one-hundred-to-one and more. In recognition of the morality factor and in particular the factors of resentment and disillusionment, the rapidly-growing US food franchise business of the 1990s, Ben and Jerry's, set a target ratio for the top salary being paid in the company to the bottom of 6:1. The Greek philosopher Plato argued that for moral and ethical reasons, in any organisation the highest paid worker should earn no more than five times the pay of the lowest paid worker. In the US in 1965, CEOs earned forty-four times the average production worker's wage; in 1996 the multiple had blown out to 212 (Pearl Meyer and Partners).

High CEO salaries are paid because the profits of the largest corporations are very large in absolute terms and so the CEO's salary is only a very small fraction of this profit. The absolute size of these large profits, in turn, is a function of concentration. The largest companies have become very large particularly by way of takeover and merger. The opportunity for such concentrating activity is part and parcel of the free-market system. An unhindered market allows for such activity, and the only way of curbing it is government intervention – hence the existence of government regulatory bodies such as the Australian Competition and Consumer Commission (ACCC).

Hence, high CEO salaries are, firstly, a function of industry concentration, which has led to very large profits (in absolute terms) thereby making very high salaries only a negligible proportion of company profits. Second, they are a function of a relatively high level of direct share ownership. The propensity for direct equity investment has increased significantly over the past decade, and shareholders are clamouring for higher returns. As a result of this pressure coming from investors, CEOs are increasingly focusing their attention on their company's share price, and are running the company with this as the chief aim; that is, the maximisation of shareholder wealth. Shareholders are satisfied to see CEOs being paid very large remuneration packages on the condition that their own wealth is increased. Consequently, there is a high and loudly voiced demand for CEOs of proven ability in managing a corporation in the interests of increasing the wealth of its shareholders. The production of a quality product for a fair and reasonable profit is a secondary aim.

Privatisation of economic activities that were once the undisputed domain of the public sector – power and water utilities particularly – is another unfortunate example of greed and therefore injustice. With these privatisations there is effectively a devaluation of the significance of the public contribution to production and a corresponding over-valuation of the contribution of the now-private owner. It is also being revealed (by the likes of corporate collapses and institutional problems) that both selfish and dishonest actions are becoming more and more commonplace and odious. Concurrent with a rise in selfish actions – a direct display of an exaggerated emphasis upon the value of the contribution of the individual – social values and actions are diminishing. However, there is such a thing as justice; its absence is keenly felt!

The consequences of *not* appropriating economic rent to the community

When the community is deprived of its natural source of income – economic rent – it has to resort to taxing income for its revenue. However, taxing personal income is theft: because it is *taking* from someone what is rightfully their own. Income (in the form of wages, salaries and profits earned from productive enterprise) belongs to the one who earned it, the one who worked for it. It is their rightful property, and to take away any of it is theft – no matter that the taking is sanctioned by man-made (un-natural) law. Hence it is unjust. "Real estate law (in the form of sanctioning the retainment of economic rent by the titleholder of land, resulting in private capital gain) has plundered the community fund and tax has plundered individual and corporate earnings" (Stewart 2008, p. 154). The community, of course, does need to have an income – but there is a natural provision for this need, and that provision is not income tax.

Our enquiry has been into the attainment of justice. It has been to seek the fundamental principle governing the just distribution of wealth between its two contributors. That principle has been discovered, and specifically, three points have emerged. In the natural order of the economic set-up:

1. There is a specific, unambiguous determinant of the just level of wages: the full value of production on the marginal site. This value belongs to the individual who worked on that site. This value is the *natural level of earnings.*

2. There is a specific, unambiguous natural source of community income: economic rent. Economic rent is the productive advantage lent to sites by the community.

3. Justice rules when each of these two sources of income goes to its rightful recipient: the full value of production upon the marginal site to the individual working on that site, economic rent to the community.

And so the answer to the question of justice in the distribution of wealth is simple. It may be stated in a single sentence: the full product of the marginal site belongs to the individual who worked on that site, and the excess production on other, better-endowed sites, belongs to the community. But the effect upon the lives of individuals and communities would be profound if wealth was distributed justly between its two contributing parties. A *just* distribution is not an *equal* distribution. An equal distribution of wealth is a distribution not in accordance with human nature, and therefore not in accordance with justice. When wealth is not distributed justly, some communities suffer the terrible problem of starvation that is rife in parts of the world today; and others, in parts of the western world (Australia, for example) – where conditions are very much better – the increasing difficulty young people are experiencing in finding employment and in attempting to buy their own home. The contribution of the community toward production in all its various forms is very large, and if collected by the community would result not only in justice (including the elimination of unemployment), but also in people as a whole enjoying the benefits of living in a wealthy community. The rightful distribution of wealth[15] is not a question of opinion. It is a question of justice, and it is the basis of ethical economics.

Justice in the distribution of wealth is important for two reasons. First,

---

[15] The foregoing is a first-principles discussion of justice in the division of wealth.
A finely-detailed discussion of this distribution – between earnings and rent – is available in *Progress and Poverty* (Henry George), Books III and IV, and *Nature of Society* (Leon MacLaren), pp. 55-59 and 175-188.

if the share of wealth going to someone who works is less than the full value of their contribution, then that is stealing. The one working is the victim of theft. Second, if the share of wealth going to someone who works is more than the value of their contribution, then *they* are committing theft. They are in receipt of the fruits of other people's labour. They are living off other people's efforts. They are in receipt of unearned income – income for which they did not contribute by way of physical or mental effort. In both situations justice is perverted, human beings suffer, and conflict of one sort or another follows.

The simultaneous existence of the very rich who have become rich through the receipt of unearned income, and the very poor, is the obvious manifestation of injustice. Being very rich through human effort is both commendable and just; being very rich through receipt of unearned income is neither commendable nor just; and being very poor in the sense of being deprived of the basics of life is neither commendable nor just. "If you want to halt the creeping plunder of your earnings, find the natural fund that runs the state ... Community value dressed up as real estate trawled huge temptations in its wake ... the seedbed of corruption" (Stewart 2008, pp. 109, 128). Whilst *equality* in the distribution of wealth is not the rule of justice,[16] great extremes in its distribution are likely to indicate the prevalence of injustice, particularly where the gap between rich and poor is growing ever larger.

... Extreme inequalities are toxic for societies but there is a body of scholarship suggesting they also cause depressions. They create a bias

---

[16] Except in the most extraordinary of situations where all participants in the productive process contribute equally to the value of the final product. "The experience of Communism has shown that the only universal medicine Marxists have for social evils – state ownership of the means of production – is not only perfectly compatible with all the disasters of the capitalist world – with exploitation, imperialism, pollution, misery, economic waste, national hatred and national oppression, but it adds to them a series of disasters of its own: inefficiency, lack of economic incentives, and above all the unrestricted rule of the omnipresent bureaucracy, a concentration of power never before known in human history ... Marxism was the greatest fantasy of our century – an idea that began in Promethean humanism and culminated in the monstrous tyranny of Stalinism" (Kolakowski 2009, p. 16).

towards asset bubbles and over-investment, while holding down consumption, until the system becomes top-heavy and tips over, as happened in the 1930s ... So we limp on, with large numbers of people trapped on the wrong side of globalisation, and nobody doing much about it. Would Franklin Roosevelt have tolerated such a state of affairs, or would he have ripped up and reshaped the global system *until it answered the needs of his citizens*? (Evans-Pritchard 2011, p. 19).

Greed manifests in many ways and has serious implications.

Rising income inequality in the United States has created political pressure for easy credit ... The top 1 per cent of households accounted for only 8.9 per cent of income in 1976, but this share grew to 23.5 per cent of the total income generated in the United States in 2007. Put differently, of every dollar of real income growth that was generated between 1976 and 2007, 58 cents went to the top 1 per cent of households. In 2007 the hedge fund manager John Paulson earned (no, was *given!*) $3.7 billion, about 74,000 times the median household income in the United States ... (Further) since the 1980s, the wages of workers at the 90th percentile of the wage distribution in the United States – such as office managers – have grown much faster than the wage of the 50th percentile worker (the median worker) – typically factory workers and office assistants (Rajan 2010, pp. 8-9).

And Brown (2011) believes that "The implications (of growing inequality) for the coherence of our societies are profound ... Containing the growth of inequality is crucial for the maintenance of the social and political structures worldwide that inhibit overt civil and military conflict"; while Day (1995, p. 66) has noted that " ... western-style capitalism, notwithstanding efforts over time to temper its excesses, appears to have no philosophical motivation other than the pursuit of profit and self-interest, and that complex revenue raising mechanisms which tax labour and enterprise appear to put a premium on evasion and deceit".

The nineteenth-century American economist Henry George was clear, direct and incisive in his lucid exposition of justice. He clearly identified the two contributors to production, clearly identified how to value the contribution of each, and thus provided the blueprint for the just distribution of wealth between the individual and the community. Likewise, the influential French economists before him, the Physiocrats; Adam Smith and John Stuart Mill; Winston Churchill; and, to the present day, Dr Ken Henry (in the 2010 Henry Review on taxation in Australia). The collection of revenue properly due to the community is effected in practice by way of a *site-value land tax*. The Henry Review (2010) strongly recommends the site-value land tax – in fact land (and natural resources) is identified in the very first recommendation of the *Review* as the basis for a "robust efficient broad-based tax". The site-value land tax, though, is not really a tax: rather, it is the collection by the community of the community's contribution toward the production of wealth. It is the public collection of publicly created economic rent. To provide for community income by way of income taxation and other such forms of taxation (including the GST) is both unnecessary and unjust. Although Hong Kong, Singapore, Denmark and Canberra (Australia) *have* adopted the site-value land tax, economies across the world are notorious for ignoring the advice of its justice. And the worst of the economic misery in the world – parts of Asia and Africa, where millions starve to death for lack of money to buy even food – exists side by side with grossly rich landlords: " ... changes of scenery from soaring wealth to slum, mansions in the midst of misery" (Stewart 2008, p. 149).

Exactly as Henry George said would happen, progress and poverty march together. It is beyond human comprehension that the dreadful economic misery that does exist in the world is allowed to continue in the face of the simple, powerful, *just* remedy being at hand. But as Stewart (2008, p. 52) has said, contemporary economics is the economics of the madhouse. Such is the price of ignorance. But we cannot say we were not told. Andrew MacLaren cried out in the British House of Commons for more than twenty years, "God gave the land to the people. Then why haven't they got it?" and Barry Jones cried out in the 1980s, "Sleepers, Wake!" "Now it's time to turn our minds to economic justice ... How can we ignore self-evident fact for petty short-term gain – politicians' votes from those who benefit from real estate gains" (Stewart 2008, pp. 60, 152).

Simplicity is a mark of truth. The natural provision for the community's income, and the natural provision for determining the level of wages – indeed, the very fact that there *are* these provisions – is further pointer to the beauty and grandeur of the natural operation of an economy.

CHAPTER 7

Justice, Land Use and the Cost of Housing

The lion's share of economic progress will always finish up being absorbed by the factor, land, as may be seen by observing the constant, steady increase in the price of land. Hence, as Henry George put it, "progress and poverty will march together". Resources flow into real estate. That fact is uncontested.

FRED HARRISON

As has been discussed in chapter 4, land is a special resource. It is special because, fundamentally, every one needs it and it has no cost of production. It is not a product. These facts are important – very important indeed.

When the site rental value of land – formally known as *economic rent* – is not appropriated to the community, but rather remains in the hands of the titleholder of the site, land takes on a price. That price is the capitalised rental value. For example, suppose that a site is occupied by a tenant who pays $12,000 per annum rent, that council rates and charges are $2,000 per annum and that the prevailing market rate of interest is 10 per cent per annum. Net site rental value appropriated by the landlord is

$10,000 per annum ($12,000 − $2,000) which, at the prevailing rate of interest gives the site a market value of $100,000. (If the interest rate were five per cent per annum the market value of the site would be $200,000).

This capitalisation of site rental value into a market price results in land becoming something that is traded in the market place, and instead of being treated as the vital substratum for all life and work, land is turned into a toy – an "investment commodity" – to be played with by investors. The consequences of this are two-fold. First, land is purchased by investors for its expected capital gain, which action is a profanity against the fundamental purpose of this primary resource: that which is *essential* for human beings to live and work on. Second, speculative activity greatly distorts the cost of a basic and fundamental need of human beings – housing.

Investors and land "developers" buy land only because they expect that its price will increase. Their purchase of land is in no way motivated by the well-being, current or future, of house dwellers! To "assist" and encourage the expected price increase to actually happen, developers *hold* land for periods of time; that is to say, they keep it off the market and allow it to sit, vacant and entirely unused, until demand for it grows such that its price rises. Then they "release" it – they allow it to be placed on the market and sold – giving the fallacious appearance of having performed a benevolent action to mankind! This whole activity of holding land and allowing it to be released and sold only when its price rises sufficiently to meet the expectations of the investor is entirely unnatural. The natural order of things is that humankind needs land to live on and to work on, and this need is generously met through the beneficence of the natural creation, in which and by which land is freely provided. Nature does not lock up land, nature does not withhold land, it simply makes it available – has always made it available – for use.

Now although in the natural order of things land is freely provided and there is sufficient in the world for every human being to live on and work on, there is also the natural tendency of people to be gregarious.

This means that there will be more than one, usually many, people who would like to occupy any one given site. Since only one can occupy a particular site at any one time, some sort of allocation process is needed to determine who that one will be. In the economic system that we are familiar with – the capitalist, free-market system, sometimes referred to as an "open-market" economy – it is the *price* of land that performs this allocation. The one who is both willing and able to pay the highest price gains occupancy.

Whilst this system of allocation "works" (it is effective), it has serious flaws. First, as has already been discussed, it is the presence of the community and its tax-funded infrastructure that gives a site its market value. Hence, payment for the right to occupy should be made to the community, not to a private individual. (Of course it needs to be remembered that while the community gives the *site* its value it does not put the capital improvements thereon – buildings and their surrounds. These are the result of individual human effort, and belong in full to the individual who worked to put them there). Second, occupation of a site by some one means that all others are excluded from it. This exclusion is not a problem in itself – there are alternative sites available. But it is a *fact* that exclusive occupancy of a site by one means that all others are excluded from it. Payment of the rental value of the site to the community may be seen as being compensation to all who are excluded – that is, everyone except the occupant of the site.

With respect to land being turned into an investment commodity, in the above example an investor is able to purchase the land (site) for $100,000 and receive rental income of $10,000 (net of rates), which represents a return on investment of 10 per cent per annum. This might appear to be an "acceptable" proposition, a harmless economic activity that causes no injustice, but the arrogation of land from being a natural resource freely provided and intended for living and working on into being an investment plaything has serious implications.

The return on the "investment" is *not* the result of any present economic activity carried out on the site *by the investor landlord.* There need be no productive activity whatsoever by the investor. He or she need contribute nothing in terms of personal exertion or anything else, but rather, simply collect the rent. Hence, as already discussed, this income is "unearned". It is the *tenant,* not the landlord, who puts the land to use and generates economic activity from which the rent ($12,000 in the above example) is paid. Proper economics asks for justice, and justice is what is rightfully *due.* What was the investor's contribution in terms of *personal exertion?* Nothing! Investment in land produces not one square inch more land or anything else (whereas investment in, say, a factory results in a building and production that did not exist previously). With respect to land, "investment" does nothing. It just decides whose name is on the title deed.

In a speech he gave in Edinburgh, Winston Churchill (1909) made plain the nature of the activity of investment in land:

> Some years ago in London there was a toll bar on a bridge across the Thames, and all the working people who lived on the south side of the river had to pay a daily toll of one penny for going and returning from their work. The spectacle of these poor people thus mulcted of so large a proportion of their earnings offended the public conscience, and agitation was set afoot, municipal authorities were roused, and at the cost of the taxpayers, the bridge was freed and the toll removed. All those people who used the bridge were saved sixpence a week, but within a very short time rents on the south side of the river were found to have risen about sixpence a week, or the amount of the toll which had been remitted!

Further, because no exertion is required of the investor in land to generate rental income, this form of investment is *attractive.* An investor can buy *more* sites, and because he or she need do nothing toward any productive activity carried out on them there is no physical limit to the number of sites that can be acquired. This is a totally different situation from that of someone in receipt of wage or salary income. Wages and salaries are only paid by an employer to those employees who are physically present and contributing to the productive process. "No work, no pay" is the ruling paradigm. Therefore it is only physically possible to hold down *one* full-time job and hence it is only physically possible to earn *one* full-time salary. Not so with investment – this physical limit does not apply.

Now the attractiveness of being able to receive unearned income cultivates a climate of greed. Because of the human failure to be greedy, the demand for investment has a tendency to be insatiable. A "successful" outcome on one investment property tends to have the effect of stimulating desire for another, and then another. In plain language, greed takes over. Adam Smith was fully aware of this when he wrote, "And hence it is that to feel much for others and little for oneself, that to restrain our selfish and to indulge our benevolent affections, constitutes the perfection of human nature". Investors want more than just one site; and people who are not already investors want to become investors. Thus the demand for sites increases and their price increases accordingly. Further, intending investors *anticipate* that site rents are going to increase over time. Based on what has happened in this country for some 200 years (much longer in other parts of the world), they are right. Site rents are likely to increase.[17] And so in assessing the price that they are prepared to pay for any given site, intending investors will estimate on the basis of expected future rents – higher rents – not current rents. Thus the market price of land is bid up by the activity of investors. Compared with the situation of land being in demand *only for its natural purpose of living and working on*, the additional demand for sites by investors bids up their price; and this

---

[17] I am not saying that land prices will *always* increase. They have, of course, decreased at certain points in time, and they probably will again. But the general tendency over a long period of time has been upward. Just ask any speculator in land if you wish to verify this point!

price is bid up even more by the fact that investors base their bid prices on expected (higher) future rents, not current rents. In other words, investors *expect* capital gain.

When land becomes subject to the profit-seeking activity of investors its naturally intended purpose is distorted and perverted. In fact, it is forgotten. Profit-seeking by investors is one thing, living is quite another. Investment in land by those not intending to live or work on the sites they purchase is not an "innocent" action. It is not an action without hurtful consequences. It forces up the price of land for those who do want to live or work on it. It forces up the cost of housing. This could not be illustrated more graphically than a research finding that intending home buyers need an after-tax income of more than $100,000 per annum ($103,000 to be precise) to be able to enter the first-home buyers market anywhere in Melbourne except on the far edges of the city's urban fringe. This is when the average level of earnings is less than half that amount, and despite one of the worst property slumps in two decades (*The Age*, 11 December 2011, p. 1). And so intending and needful house buyers face financial stress and/or exclusion from the housing market.

A core purpose of economics is to ensure that everyone has access to the land which they need for life, and that this access is equitable, is just. The primary interest of investors is profit. It is not whether or not every-one has access to the land they need, on terms they can afford. If holding land out of use is expedient with respect to increasing its price – capital gain – then the investor will do this. He or she is not concerned with the fact that this action is depriving someone of the present *use* of that land. That deprivation is the concern of the true economist, not the investor. Land has only one function in the affairs of mankind: to be used. Invest-ment activity is not interested in this function. The dual effect of land being turned over to investors – its price being forced up and a frequent withholding of it from use – has a serious, harmful and hurtful effect upon those who simply need it to live.

The cost of *houses* has actually been falling

The cost of housing is an important private and social issue. And, as is well appreciated, the cost of housing has risen to record levels in recent years, putting it in the unaffordable category for some and placing stress and anxiety on many others due to high mortgage repayments. However, the cost of *houses* has been *falling,* and falling for very many years.

The "cost of housing", as the expression is commonly used and understood, consists of two components: the cost of the building and the cost of the land on which the building stands. It is the latter cost that has risen, not the former. The cost of the building has been falling – due to increased efficiency and technological advances in the building industry. But this fall has been swamped by the rising price of the land on which the building stands. **To miss this point leads to a total misunderstanding of this most important issue,** and therefore an inability to deal with what is now a pressing social problem: the very high proportion of average earnings needed to "put a roof over one's head", and consequently, the small proportion of earnings left to spend on all the other necessities of life. The irony of this situation is that land, the increase in price of which is the whole substance of this problem, has a cost of production of *zero*. It is *given* to the human race, for our use and enjoyment. But the fact of this great gift is ignored, utterly ignored, and human beings charge each other a price – a distressingly high price – for access to this gift! But Shakespeare did say, "Man, proud man ... plays such fantastic tricks before high heaven as make the angels weep"!

Investment in the likes of roads, ports, parks, schools, is a productive activity. Investment in land creates nothing. Any land being "invested in" was in existence long before investment in it was ever thought of, continues to be in existence quite independently of and with total disregard for investment in it, and will continue to be in existence long thereafter. In the most succinct terms possible, 'land *is*'. It exists. It is not brought into existence – by investment or any other means. The only question, then, is one of allocating it amongst "competing" users or occupants and providing security of tenure to the occupant. Security of tenure is necessary that the occupant – the tenant – may have peace of mind that his or her tenure will not be terminated arbitrarily; and that any improvements made to or upon the site and any production upon it will be the rightful, defendable property of the tenant. This is the function of economics with respect to land: to allocate sites amongst a competing population of users, to protect property rights of tenants who improve the site or produce thereon, and to ensure that the rental value of the site is paid to the community. Full payment of site rental value to the community would **eliminate land being subject to capital gain,** and therefore eliminate land from being a target of investment activity.

The real issue with regard to the prohibitive cost of housing is the **prohibitive cost of land.** It has been pushed to socially harmful heights, which situation is becoming increasingly recognised. *The Economist* (March 2011) reports that housing in Australia is 53 per cent overvalued. What madness, what human folly: something that is given us *for free* now being sold back to us at distressingly high prices! Former governor of the Reserve Bank of Australia, Ian MacFarlane (2011, p. 11), said: "Why has the price of an entry-level new home gone up as much as it has? Why is it not like it was when ... we were able to buy a block of land very cheaply and put a house upon it very cheaply? Why is that not available? Why is that not the case now?" Since it is natural that land has been provided free of charge it must be that an un-natural factor(s) has changed this great freedom. This factor is the allowing of site rental value to be appropriated by individuals instead of being paid to that which gives rise to it – the community.

The harmful and hurtful effects of the arrogation of purpose that is a consequence of permitting land to become an investment commodity cannot be over-estimated. Investment in land causes the price of land to be higher – very much higher – than it would be in the absence of investment demand. Monetary policy (i.e. movement in interest rates) is closely linked here, because its effect can be opposite to that intended. In the case of the pronounced 2006 – 2008 slowdown in US economic activity,

> ... the Federal Reserve went into overdrive, cutting interest rates sharply. By doing so, it sought to energize activity in sectors of the economy that are interest sensitive ... Instead, the low interest rates prompted US consumers to buy houses, which in turn raised house prices and led to a surge in housing investment. A significant portion of the additional demand came from segments of the population with low credit ratings or impaired credit histories ... who now obtained access to credit that had hitherto been denied them. Moreover, rising house prices gave subprime borrowers the ability to keep refinancing into low interest rate mortgages (thus avoiding default) ... For many, the need to repay loans seemed remote and distant ... The gravy train eventually came to a halt after the Federal Reserve raised interest rates and halted the house price rise that had underpinned the frenzied lending (Rajan 2010, pp. 5-6).

As has been said already, the opportunity of getting unearned income turns investors greedy. Adam Smith was well aware of the propensity of the human being to be greedy, so were the ancient scriptures. *The Bhagavad Gita* is plain about the problem of greed: it uses the expression, " ... blinded by greed", (ch. 1, Hodgkinson trans.). Under the influence of greed, the investor loses perspective as to his or her own real, actual, material needs. The accumulation of money is pursued as an end in itself. The investor is also blinded to the needs of others. Escalating land (and therefore housing) prices are stretching family budgets to and beyond breaking point, resulting in some being homeless or housed in sub-stand-ard conditions, and many living under financial stress and its associated strained human relationships. But this is looked upon by investors (and some economists) as being an unfortunate but "unavoidable" happening.

Well, it is **not** unavoidable. It is entirely avoidable. Indeed, it is entirely unnecessary. However, property investors are not interested in hearing this. They are not interested in the fact that more than one in four Victorians, for example, are in receipt of welfare payments of one kind or another (*Herald Sun,* 21 March 2011, p.1). "When easy money comes into contact with the profit motive of a sophisticated, competitive, and amoral financial sector, a deep fault line develops" (Rajan 2010, p. 9). Property investors, taken as a whole, are amoral. They are interested only in the price of land increasing, without any consideration for the effect this has on other people who are simply trying to live on it.

Investment in land, at the *individual* level, is not the problem. The cessation of investment by one individual would not solve the problem (of high land and therefore high housing costs). It is property investment *en masse* that is the problem.

> There are deep fault lines in the global economy, fault lines that have developed because in an integrated economy and in an integrated world, what is best for the individual actor or institution is not always best for the system ... The flood of money lapping at the doors of borrowers originated, in part, from investors far away who had earned it by exporting to the United States and feeding the national consumption habit ... This is where the sophisticated U.S. financial sector stepped in. Securitization dealt with many of these concerns. If the mortgage was packaged together with mortgages from other areas, diversification would reduce the risk ... The U.S. financial sector thus bridged the gap between an overconsuming and overstimulated United States and an underconsuming, understimulated rest of the world. But this entire edifice rested on the housing market ... rising house prices provided the home equity to refinance old loans and finance new consumption ... The world was in a sweet but unsustainable spot (Rajan 2010, pp. 4, 6).

The solution lies in removing altogether the opportunity, indeed the possibility, of land being an investment good. This requires appropriate action at *government* (not individual) level. It requires appropriate law with respect to the terms of occupancy of land. Informing government in this respect is the prime function of economics. "Good economics cannot be divorced from good politics: this is why the field of economics was formerly known as political economy" (Rajan 2010, p. 19).

Land is provided in order that life on this earth is possible. Housing without access to land is impossible. Housing with access only to very expensive land – made expensive only by artificial forces – makes housing very expensive, and this makes life very difficult for many, very difficult indeed.

Chapter 8

Credit and the Real Nature of Money

A precondition for becoming head of the Federal Reserve or other
financial agency is that the candidate not *understand how*
banking works.

John Kenneth Galbraith

"Credit" is commonly thought of as being the provision of a loan. A question asked by shoppers, for example, is, "Is credit available?" meaning, can the goods be paid for later? However, although this is how credit is perceived commonly, this perception is a distortion of its real meaning. This distortion causes the real meaning – in the context of banking and finance – to be hidden from view.

The word *credit* comes from the Latin *credere* – to believe, and the dictionary definition of *credit* is, "the quality of being believable or trustworthy". The obvious question, then, is: "What is it that is to be believed?" This is an important question, in fact *the* important question, the answer to which lies at the heart of understanding the real meaning and nature of credit. According to the *Random House Dictionary,* credit is "confidence in a purchaser's ability and intention to pay".

When an individual *seeks* credit, he or she makes a promise to repay that credit. To *give* credit is to believe, to trust, that the person seeking it will fulfil this promise. As is well understood, in order to be given credit a promise or "guarantee" has to be given by the seeker. The real meaning of credit, then, is that a person making a promise is "given credit" for being believable. The person is acknowledged as *being believable,* is credited with being believable – in the sense of the old saying, "Give credit where it is due".

The present context in which credit is being considered is, of course, the context of economics. In the context of economics the proper realm of credit is the financing, or "funding", of the production of goods or services that are to be marketed upon the completion of production. The purpose of credit is to bridge the time gap between the commencement of production and the receipt of funds from sale of the product. In an imaginary world where production and sale were instantaneous events, with no time gap between them, credit would not be needed – indeed, would not exist. However, in practical matters as things now stand, the producer must fund certain necessary expenditures, such as purchase of raw materials and payment of wages, and the function of credit is to provide for these payments which must be made prior to proceeds being available from sale of the product. Sale of the product provides the funds to repay, or extinguish, the obligation incurred by the recipient of credit.

The proper context of credit in economics, then, is expected production. Real credit applies to and operates in the realm of the production of goods and services that are anticipated but have not yet materialised. To seek credit in the context of expected production involves making a promise, and the promise is that the recipient will pay back that credit. To be able to fulfil this promise the recipient of credit needs to produce the said good or service and sell it in the market place, thereby generating sufficient funds to repay the "loan". But, first and foremost, it must be noted that the essence of giving credit is *not* the granting of a loan. It is the granting to the seeker of credit the status of being believable with respect to what he or she is promising to *do*. Nor is credit the granting of a loan from some pre-existing stock of funds ("deposits"); nor is credit money. Credit and money are two different things (as will be discussed shortly). Credit is the belief that someone seeking a "loan" will actually "produce the goods", can be trusted to produce. To be given credit is to be trusted.

One way of looking at credit is that it is the debiting of a producing customer's account in the belief that that account will be credited upon future receipt of proceeds from the sale of the product. Thus, credit is, in a sense, a "double action", a cycle: the giving of it, and then its return or extinguishment (the return commonly being called "repayment"). In accounting terminology the issue and extinguishment of credit involves two offsetting book entries. This will be illustrated shortly with a specific, simplified example. For purposes of simplicity (and obvious applicability) it will be assumed that the issuer of credit is a bank.

Money, credit and trust

The granting (issue) of credit must be matched by production, otherwise there will be inflation. Money – new money – is created each time a bank grants credit, and is "destroyed" upon payment back to the bank of the amount originally granted. Thus, with each new round of production financed by credit there is a cycle, or process, of the creation and destruction of money. The creation of money is consequent upon an intention to produce and the corresponding granting of credit, and with the sale of the product and repayment to the bank comes the destruction of money. It is a flow process, a situation of flux. New money arises at the commencement of the productive process and ceases to be at the conclusion of that process. This will be illustrated in the simplified example to follow.

However, the *essence* of credit is not money. It is trust – trust in the capacity of the one who seeks credit to fulfil the necessary promise: the promise to produce and thereby repay. Money does arise out of the process of credit, but this money is not, itself, credit. It is a lubricant, a marvellously-effective lubricant that smooths and makes easy the transactions of the market-place. But the distinction between credit and money is an important distinction – a very important distinction.

There is an old story that is relevant as a pointer to the underlying principle of the real nature of credit, money and trust. This story highlights the origin of what is known today as "fractional reserve banking". This is the story told to schoolchildren as to how the idea and concept of what we now know as "banking" arose. The story begins with a holder of newly-found gold (whom we will call a *miner*) wanting somewhere safe to keep the precious metal and going to the local goldsmith who, by reason of his trade, happens to have a "safe" on his premises for the purpose of storing gold and other valuables. The miner hands over the gold to the goldsmith for safe storage and in return the goldsmith gives the miner a *certificate* – a receipt for the gold that has been deposited with him. This is step one of the story.

Some time later the miner wants to buy a horse, and so he goes to the goldsmith and withdraws a quantity of gold sufficient to pay for the horse. The miner gives this gold to the horse dealer and takes possession of the horse. The horse dealer then goes back to the goldsmith (since they live in the same locality) and deposits the gold (and obtains a receipt for doing so). The goldsmith, once again, has in his safe the original quantity of gold. Next the miner wants to buy some building materials and so goes to the goldsmith to withdraw enough gold to pay the town's builder. The gold is handed over by the miner to the builder in exchange for the materials, and the builder then takes the gold to the goldsmith for safe storage and is given a receipt. Once again the goldsmith is left with the original quantity of gold in his safe. This is step two of the story.

The goldsmith, after having been witness to the several acts of gold being taken out of his safe and subsequently returned, now realises that there is no need for the physical withdrawal and re-depositing of gold. He, the goldsmith, is trusted in the community, and accordingly, any receipts he issues for holdings of gold are deemed by the community to be reliable. In other words, the receipt held by the miner for the original deposit of gold is trusted; that is to say, people of the community believe that the miner *does actually possess* the quantity of gold specified on his deposit receipt. Hence, instead of the miner withdrawing physical gold to pay for the horse and then the horse dealer subsequently re-depositing that same amount of gold, the goldsmith realises that he can issue a "receipt" – certificate of ownership – for that same amount of gold in the name of the horse dealer, and the horse dealer be given this receipt in exchange for the horse. Likewise with the purchase of building materials, the miner can give to the builder a receipt obtained from the goldsmith for that amount of gold that will pay for the building materials.

What has happened is that the miner, when he wishes to make payment for a purchase, realises that he can simply hand over his *receipt* for gold in the goldsmith's safe – without the trouble of actually going to get the physical gold and handing that over. This also suits the horse dealer and the builder (and anyone else in the community with whom the miner wishes to do business) since they do not have to go to the trouble of visiting the goldsmith either. The exchange of receipts for deposits of gold, rather than the exchange of physical gold itself, becomes commonplace. This is step three of the story.

Notice, the gold is never actually used! The physical, natural substance, gold, is not used. It *does* serve the purpose of being the *source* of the original receipt and it gives that receipt its "backing", its intrinsic value; and it gives validity to the value of any subsequent receipts issued by the goldsmith. But the point is that the trade of the community takes place without the exchange of physical gold (and, ultimately, irrespective of its existence). The real activity of the economy is the exchange of the goods and services needed by its members. The essential component in this flow of trade is *trust* – not physical gold. When the horse dealer hands over the horse to the miner in exchange for a certificate (receipt) specifying a quantity of gold equal in value to the agreed-upon value of the horse, he is trusting that the goldsmith (the issuer of the receipt) does have that quantity of gold in his safe; likewise when the builder accepts a receipt for gold equal in value to that of the building materials given to the miner. Thus, withdrawing and then re-depositing the physical gold is unnecessary, and the key to this is *trust* – trust that what is written on a receipt issued by the goldsmith *is* actually in his safe (in the form of gold).

For purposes of a practical illustration of the meaning and implications of credit, let us assume a highly simplified model economy engaged in the manufacture and sale of woollen jumpers. The community consists of ten members. Three farmers graze sheep from which come fleeces of wool – the raw material for the manufacture of the jumpers. Manufacturing will take place in a factory employing four people. A retail shop, employing two people, will purchase the finished jumpers from the factory and retail them to the community. A bank, employing one banker, exists as assessor and provider of credit. Thus our economy of ten consists of: three farmers, four factory workers, two retailers, and a banker. All ten will need, and will purchase, a woollen jumper.

The three farmers tend their sheep and produce ten fleeces of wool, which they sell to the factory for $3 per fleece. For purposes of simplification it will be assumed that growing wool is an entirely naturally occurring event with zero out-of-pocket costs of production. The sheep live, and indeed thrive, on the naturally grown grass. Hence, the inputs to the production of the wool are the farmers' labour and the bounties of nature.

Now it will be assumed that the factory manager has no cash – no money – with which to buy the required fleeces of wool, nor has he any cash with which to pay the four (including himself) factory workers, and so he goes to the bank seeking credit. He will ask for a credit facility to the value of $70, calculated as follows: ten fleeces at $3 each plus wages of $10 for each of the four factory workers. His promise will be to manufacture and sell ten woollen jumpers, and thereby repay the amount of

$70, plus a charge for the bank's service of receiving and assessing his application for credit. The credit charge is for *the service of establishing the credit-worthiness* of the applicant. It is *not* interest. Repayment of the $70 plus credit-establishment charge will be upon sale of the manufactured jumpers.

In deciding whether or not the factory manager is worthy of being granted credit, the banker will have to decide in his or her own mind the technical and financial viability of the factory manager's proposition: to "borrow" $70 to be used as just outlined, and repaid upon completion of the manufacturing process. In assessing the viability of the proposal the banker will first check the work being done by the farmers, to make sure that there is every reasonable prospect of the said ten fleeces of suitable wool being available to the factory when needed, at the price of $3 per fleece. In the process of making this assessment the banker will inspect the condition of the farm, see that sheep in the required number are physically present, and satisfy himself of the farmers' ability and knowledge necessary for the production of wool. The bank manager will then ascertain the suitability of the factory and its workers for the manufacture of the jumpers; and finally, will satisfy himself that there will be a retail outlet for them; i.e. that there will be a genuine demand for ten woollen jumpers upon completion of the manufacturing process. The factory plans on selling the ten finished jumpers to the retail shop, at the wholesale price of $7.50 each, and the retail price to final customers will be $10.

The work of ascertaining the credit-worthiness of the factory manager who has applied for credit to the value of $70 is the real and substantial work of the bank manager, and it is the provision of this service for which the bank makes a charge. Let us assume that the banker is satisfied with the factory manager's credit application – satisfied that there exists, firstly in the farmers, and then in the factory manager and his team, the competency, skill, entrepreneurship and responsibility to ensure that ten fleeces of wool and ten jumpers, respectively, of suitable quality will be farmed and then manufactured within the appropriate time interval and be ready for wholesale to the retailer who, in turn, can be trusted to make payment for same. Upon being satisfied with the proposal the banker will agree to giving credit to the manager for the amount of $70. The bank will then print $70 in notes and issue these notes to the factory manager. The account of the factory with the bank will be debited $75 – a simple book entry. This amount will consist of the $70 requested plus a $5 service charge for the banker's work of assessing credit-worthiness. The factory manager will then use the $70 in notes as follows: payment to the three farmers of $30 (ten fleeces at $3 per fleece), and payment of wages to the four factory workers of $10 each, total wages $40; total payments $70. The bank will also raise its own "employee wages" account, debit it for the amount of $5 and print $5 in notes to be given to the bank manager as his or her wages for credit services provided.

The retailer (two salespeople) now wants to purchase, wholesale, the ten jumpers from the factory but, like the factory manager previously, has no cash in hand and will need to rely on credit for purchase of the stock. Hence the retailer will approach the banker for a "line of credit", for the amount of $95: purchase of ten jumpers at $7.50 each, total $75; and payment of wages to the two retailer workers, $10 each, total wages $20.

Again, let us assume that the banker agrees to give credit to the retailer, for the amount of $95. Before agreeing, the banker would have carried out all the necessary and appropriate checks to determine whether or not he should believe in the retailer's proposal; i.e. whether he could trust the retailer to conduct the business of making the purchase of jumpers and then retailing them at a sufficient profit to allow for full and timely repayment of the loan. Part of the check carried out by the banker would be an inspection of the factory to see if the jumpers were being, or had been, manufactured, to an acceptably high standard; part of the check would be an inspection of the retail outlet to determine whether it was attractive and serviceable to prospective customers, and whether the retailer him-self was presentable, responsible and trustworthy; and part of the check would be to establish whether, indeed, there would be sufficient demand in the community for woollen jumpers such that the retailer could sell all of his intended stock, at the proposed retail price. In this regard the banker would note that there was a total of ten people in the community (three farmers, four factory workers, two retail salespeople and one bank-er), all of whom would need a jumper; and he would be aware of the long-range weather forecast being for a cold forthcoming winter. All these several aspects of checking the validity of the retailer's application for credit involve the banker coming to an assessment of the commercial trustworthiness of the retailer and his proposal. The ability to do this would be assisted greatly by the banker having first-hand knowledge of the community in which both he and the retailer operated.

The request for credit having been agreed to – $95 in amount – the bank will print notes to this value and give same to the retail manager. Concurrently the bank will further debit its "employee wages" account by the amount of $5, for credit services provided by its manager to the retailer, and print $5 in notes to be given to the manager. The bank manager will, then, at this time, be in receipt of the total amount of $10 for banking services provided. The retail manager, who has just been given credit to the value of $95, will pay out this amount (in notes) as follows: $75 to the factory for purchase of the 10 jumpers at $7.50 each, and $20 ($10 each) to the two retailers. The factory manager will thus be in receipt of $75 and will pay this money into its account with the bank, the balance of which would have been $75[18] debit. This account will now be cleared (will have zero balance). From the bank's perspective, the factory will have cleared its debt in full, and the bank will have earned a fee of $5 for its credit-facility service.

---

[18] $70 line of credit sought plus $5 bank service charge for credit assessment.

The retailer has been granted credit for $95, and with the bank charging a service fee – $5 – for assessing the retailer's credit-worthiness, the retailer's account with the bank will have a debit balance of $100.

The retailer now proceeds to sell his or her stock of ten jumpers, at the price of $10 each. As it is wintertime and cold, all ten people of the economy will require a warm woollen jumper, and all will buy one. The three farmers (who sold ten fleeces of wool at $3 per fleece) each will have earned $10 for his service of being a farmer – for providing the raw material for the jumpers. They each spend their earnings in the purchase of a jumper. The four factory workers were each paid $10 in wages for working in the factory: they will spend their wages each on the purchase of a jumper. The two retailers were paid a wage of $10 each: they, too, will spend their wages on the purchase of a jumper. And finally the banker will have earned a fee for service of $10 – $5 from each of the two parties whose creditworthiness was assessed – and will spend his or her earnings on the purchase of a jumper. Thus, the retailer will be in receipt of a total of $100, which amount he or she will pay to the bank, thereby clearing in full the debit balance of $100.

The bank, thus, will have received back a total of $175 in notes ($75 from the factory and $100 from the retailer) as a consequence of these two parties repaying their debt. It had printed a total of $175 ($70 for the factory, $95 for the retailer and $10 for its manager). Thus all of the money that was printed and circulated will be back with the bank. It can then either shred these notes or store them for re-use at the next round of credit-facilitated production.

The cycle of production and the creation of money
A full cycle of production will now have been completed. The real outcome of this cycle of activity is that all the members of the community will be in possession of a woollen jumper – the output of their activity – and will, therefore, be able to enjoy the fruit of their labour. In fact, the

end result of our economic model is two-fold. First, everyone obtained a woollen jumper. Second, and importantly, in the process of this happening all were gainfully employed. Throughout the chain of economic activity that took place, money served an important purpose: it provided a smoothly-flowing and readily-accepted method of giving to each participant in the productive process the "power", the ability, to participate in the consumption of its output.

The economy commenced the cycle of production with no money. Credit was issued along the way – at two strategic points – and book entries made accordingly. The physical money (notes) used to facilitate the free flow of the stages of production was created (printed) and issued by the bank to the appropriate parties. Credit, given first to the factory, and then to the retailer was accompanied by the printing of notes. At the completion of the cycle all of the money printed by the bank had been returned to its source. It had served its purpose. Money had been created (upon the granting of credit) and then withdrawn to its source, via being spent on the output of the production for which credit had been granted.

The *real* function of the banker

The function of banker is vital to the proper operation of credit. That function is to ensure that credit is matched by production. If planned production fails to materialise, then the money created by the granting of credit is valueless. It is valueless because it has no "backing" – there is no production to "back it up". The result is inflation. The giving of credit is the giving of trust: trust that the production promised by the seeker of credit will be forthcoming. In giving credit the banker has established that he or she can trust that the money so created will be backed by production. This is the crux of the work of the banker. It is the skill and judgement necessary to foresee those situations where there is every probability that the proposed production associated with an application for credit will be forthcoming, as against those situations where it is unlikely to be forthcoming. Thus, special skill is required of a banker. The real banker grants credit in order to facilitate expected production, and in doing so takes a risk – but a calculated risk. The *modern-day* "banker" grants loans, not credit, and takes out a mortgage over the borrower's property to cover the bank's risk. The latter is a totally different proposition from the former. The real banker has a skilful, demanding job!

The skill required of a banker – to be able to establish the credit-worthiness of a seeker of credit – is considerable and not widely possessed. As already said, essentially it is the art of being able to determine whether or not a potential borrower should be trusted, whether he or she can be, should be, believed. It is the ability to assess the practical viability of proposed productive ventures, and this assessment requires skilful judgement. The traditional – as distinct from the contemporary – banker, whose task it was to do just that, in fact required the skills to assess *two* characteristics of seekers of credit: the practical, commercial viability of the relevant business proposition, and the personal trustworthiness and integrity of the applicant. Possession by an individual of the skill to assess one of these characteristics, let alone both together, is not as common as might at first be thought. These two characteristics of seekers of credit are, of course, related. A trustworthy seeker of credit is unlikely to present a commercially flawed business case to a banker. The business quality and viability of the proposition for which credit is being sought will be an indicator of the personal character of the seeker. However, it is possible for a weak, untrustworthy character to present a good business plan, and it is possible that a trustworthy character will present a commercially unviable business plan. Hence the true banker needs both the skill of being able to judge commercial viability and the skill of being able to judge personal trustworthiness.

In order to avoid the considerable difficulty and embarrassing ramifications involved in a banker *not* possessing these skills, contemporary banking practice resorts to legally "securing" a loan. Trust is abandoned, and is replaced with an enforceable right. Rather than trust the seeker of credit, modern banking practice is to secure a mortgage over his or her property. Thus there is reliance not upon trust but upon legal remedy. The seeker of credit – the borrower – is not trusted, but rather is tied up in a binding legal agreement to repay the funds or have his or her property sold by the bank in order to recover the debt. If the business venture for which credit has been granted fails, the bank has the power to sell property and recoup the amount of the loan. Given the availability of this power to recoup, banks need not be as concerned about establishing the creditworthiness of borrowers as they would be in the case of true credit, where the sole criterion for and source of security is the establishment by the bank of the commercial viability of the proposal for which credit is sought. The contemporary bank, thus, is not vitally concerned with the borrower meeting promised production, because if this doesn't happen then the bank simply forecloses on the borrower's property. Trust is not required on the part of the bank. Instead, it relies on an irrefutable claim over the borrower's property.

Interest and *usury*

There is another serious departure by contemporary banking from its proper function of providing credit. Contemporary banking does not seem to believe in the ability of a bank to create money. Rather, it is conducted on the premise that a loan may be made only out of, from, a pre-existing stock of funds. This view denies the function of true credit, and relies on – in fact demands – the pre-existence of a stock of funds, an essential component of which is deposits. Depositors are paid a rate of interest to make and maintain deposits, and borrowers – seekers of "credit" – are charged a rate of interest on money borrowed from these deposits. This is not credit at all in the real meaning of the word: "to believe, to trust". Further, the charging of interest is not part of the provision of true credit. Interest is neither justified nor necessary in the granting of true credit. The money required to facilitate the productive process for which credit is sought has no cost of production – except, in the case of the use of notes,[19] the cost of operating the printing press; and the cost of book-keeping in the case of the use of electronic means. A *service charge* for the work of assessing the credit-worthiness of the seeker of credit is both legitimate and necessary, but not the levying of interest.

Money is created "by the stroke of a pen", not by human work effort, and so interest is unjust. It is unearned income to those who receive it, and an unjust cost for those who have to pay it. In the story of true credit the only work effort involved is the service of assessing the credit-worthiness of the seeker of credit. There is no work effort involved in the creation of money (other than "the stroke of a pen" or the pressing of the printing machine button). This is why interest has been referred to in history as "usury". This is why interest is forbidden in Islamic commerce.

Barter and what it reveals

There is another way our simple economy could have operated. It could have operated without any money at all. This would have been a practical possibility. All of the participants could have agreed at the outset of the cycle of production that they would make their various contributions of skill and effort on the basis that they would then *wait*, to receive a woollen jumper upon the *completion* of the productive process. The farmers' contribution to the productive process would be the supply of the necessary quantity and quality of fleece wool; the contribution of the factory workers would be the turning of the wool into jumpers; and the retailers would see to the timely and efficient delivery of them to their rightful claimants – the various participants in the productive process.

This reference to an economy without money (commonly known, of

---

[19] Alternatives are the issue of a cheque book (and payments would be made to employees and farmers by cheque); or electronic card.

course, as a barter economy) is not made to imply or suggest in any way whatsoever that the absence of money is a preferred way of operating. To the contrary. As is well known and has long been understood, money is a lubricant to the productive cycle and its use introduces an ease, flexibility and efficiency to the economic process. The reference to a moneyless economy is to reveal two important facts.

First, in the absence of money there is the requirement of *trust* by participating members of the economy. This trust is that each believes that the other will do as he or she promised toward the agreed economic activity. The result of each doing as he or she promised is that the agreed-upon product will manifest, in a timely manner and suitable quality. Trust is the essence of the operation of a moneyless economy, and the reason trust is needed is the simple fact that each contributor to the economic process will have to wait until the final product is available for use. Of all the economic agents – the participants in the production of the woollen jumpers – farmers will have to wait the longest between the time of providing their input to the productive process and their receipt of the finished product; retailers will have the shortest wait. Trust bridges the *time gap* – the gap between when the farmers hand over their wool to the factory and when the finished jumpers are ready for wear.

To repeat, the point of the immediate discussion is *not* the recommendation of a return to the practice of barter – the exchange of one good (human intelligence and labour in this case) for another (a woollen jumper) – even though **this exchange is precisely what is happening** in our model economy (and in **all** economies). What is being discussed is *waiting:* waiting in trust that the promised product will come to fruition. The parties concerned wait for the final product to be delivered after having *first* made their productive inputs. This preparedness to wait is *trust.* In the customary situation of an economy adopting the use of money, each participant in that economy receives a monetary payment at the time he or she makes the contribution toward production. They still have to wait for the finished product to be available – the time gap is there just the same – but they have money in their hand in the meantime, and thus do not perceive themselves to be relying on trust. They perceive themselves to have *been paid* for their efforts (which they have been, of course). But, equally it needs to be noted that in having *been paid,* they do not yet have possession of the physical fruits of their labour – a woollen jumper.

The real nature of money

The second important fact revealed by considering a moneyless economy is that money is no "real" thing. Aside from the fact that it is not something we can eat or wear, it is not something that contributes physically to the productive process. It can be created at will by the stroke of a pen or the rolling of the printing press. When money is present (i.e. when it is part of the functioning of the economy) it has no effect whatsoever, for better or for worse, on **what is actually happening**: the mental and physical activities involved in the production of the required good or service. When it is absent (i.e. in a barter economy), likewise its absence has no effect whatsoever on what is actually happening: the mental and physical activities involved in the production of the required good or service. Thus, money has no real effect – and therefore, in truth, it is never a limiting factor in the productive process. Its absence does not, for example, stop sheep from growing wool. Sheep do not produce wool because they are paid to. Growth of wool is a natural, physically occurring phenomenon. Also in the case of the factory: its output is the direct result of the activity of men and machines. If *they* were absent production would stop. It is *their* present activity, not money, which is the cause of production. Money may appear to be the reason that the men and women workers come to the factory in the first place, but it is not the money that is responsible for the output of the product. If men and women come *because of* money, this is only because they are not prepared to wait for the receipt of the final product. That is to say, they are not willing to be participants in a barter economy. Thus, to say that money is an essential factor in production is to misunderstand the nature of money. It is to take it to be a real, limiting factor of production when in fact it is not. What *is* real in the act of production is *work*, and work is a natural function of the human being, not an outcome delivered through the agency of money. An obvious verification of this fact is to witness the prodigious physical output from people attending upon their unpaid hobbies and sports. A serious consequence of the misunderstanding of the nature of money is that *new projects that could be started are not started because of* **the belief that there is no money** *available.*

Conventional wisdom has it that printing money is inflationary – that *any* printing of money is inflationary. It is not. Printing money may be inflationary, but it need not be. It depends: it depends on why the money is printed. Printing of money is not inflationary if it is backed by production – that is, if the money is being printed in response to new production of the same value. It is the job of the real banker to ensure that this happens – that new money is printed only as a consequence of promised new production – and, therefore, that printing money does not result in inflation. Granting of credit and printing new money are sequential events. When this fundamental function of banking – the assessment of creditworthiness – is forgotten or ignored, then printing money *is* likely to result in inflation. But the remedy, the wise course of action, is not to stop printing money. It is to restore the genuine banker.

Rajan (2010) seems to understand proper banking:

> ... So did no one care about credit quality? The investment banks ... did care, after a fashion. To sell mortgages on, they had to satisfy themselves that the underlying credit quality was sound. In the past, when a bank made a mortgage loan that it intended to hold on its books, it called the prospective borrower in. The loan officer interviewed him, sought documents verifying employment and income, and assessed

whether the borrower was able and willing to carry the debt. **These assessments were not just based on hard facts; they also included judgement calls such as whether the borrower seemed well mannered, cleanly attired, trustworthy, and capable of holding a job.** Cultural cues such as whether the applicant had a firm handshake or looked the loan officer in the eye when answering questions no doubt played a role ... many of these judgement calls did seem to add value to credit evaluations. So did the loan officer's knowledge that his client would be back to haunt his conscience if he put him in an unaffordable house.

But as investment banks put together gigantic packages of mortgages, the judgement calls became less and less important in credit assessments ... Indeed, recording judgement calls in a way that could not be supported by hard facts might have opened the mortgage lender to lawsuits alleging discrimination. All that seemed to matter to the investment banks and the rating agencies were the numerical credit score of the borrower and the amount of the loan relative to house value. These were hard pieces of information that could be processed easily and that ostensibly summarised credit quality. Accordingly, the brokers who originated loans focused on nothing else. Indeed, as the market became red-hot, they no longer even bothered to verify employment or income. Part-time gardeners became tree surgeons purportedly earning in the middle six figures annually.

The judgement calls historically made by loan officers were, in fact, extremely important to the overall credit assessment. As they were dispensed with, the quality of mortgage-origination decisions deteriorated, even though the hard numbers continued to look good ... It really does matter if the borrower is rude, shifty, and slovenly in the loan interview, for it says something about his capacity to hold a job, no matter what his credit score indicates ... New Century Financial (founded in 1995, went public 1997) eventually filed for bankruptcy

... said in a news release announcing the company's bankruptcy ... that it had 'helped millions of Americans, many who might not otherwise have been able to access credit or to realise the benefits of home ownership'. The company neglected to mention that for millions of these homeowners, their houses were like millstones around their necks, drowning them in a sea of debt (pp. 128-129).

Rajan explains, further, how poor banking practice led to severe problems:

Politicians love to have banks expand housing credit, for credit achieves many goals at the same time. It pushes up house prices, making households feel wealthier, and allows them to finance more consumption ... And everything is safe – as safe as houses – at least for a while. Easy credit has large, positive, immediate, and widely distributed benefits, whereas the costs all lie in the future .... easy credit masked the problems caused by easy credit – until house prices stopped rising and the flood of defaults burst forth ... Too many poor families who should never have been lured into buying a house have been evicted after losing their meagre savings and are now homeless; too many houses have been built that will not be lived in ... Although home ownership rates did go up – from 64 per cent of households in 1994 to 69 per cent in 2004 – too many households that could not afford to borrow were induced to do so, and since 2004 home ownership has declined steadily – to 67 per cent, 2009 – with the rate likely to fall further as many households face foreclosure ... Cynically as it may seem, easy credit has been used as a palliative throughout history by governments that are unable to address the deeper anxieties of the middle class directly ... In the United States, the expansion of home ownership – a key element of the American dream – to low- and middle-income households was the defensible linchpin for the broader aims of expanding credit and consumption (pp. 8-9, 31, 44).

The true banker's function is the establishment of creditworthiness. The true banker's function is to judge and decide upon when the printing of money is inflationary and when it is not. Interest has no place in real credit. The charging of interest is the consequence of not understanding credit and not understanding the real nature of money.

CHAPTER 9

Economic Freedom: the forgotten state

Where society is so conducted that many men and women are precluded from choosing an occupation suited to their particular talents, the desire to live and to live more fully, which moves so strongly in each of them, may run perverse and impel them to frustration and defeat. Fear of unemployment or of the orders of government is an inversion of the desire to live. It will drive a human being into employment in which his genius cannot grow but must be limited and confined. Thus trapped, he may seek his freedom in many ways.

Leon MacLaren

A casual observer of economic affairs in the western world today may be of the opinion that economic freedom is the prevailing state of affairs – that we *do have* economic freedom. Official statistics tell us that there is close to full employment, consumer spending is high, standards of housing almost everywhere are at least satisfactory and in many cases luxurious, and the typical lifestyle appears to be relaxed and inclusive of many hours of leisure time. Hence, the appearance is of economic freedom, and a high degree of it at that, particularly if the observer himself or herself is a well-paid executive. But deeper observation and enquiry reveal otherwise.

Civilisation rests upon *two* great freedoms: civil freedom and economic freedom. Economic freedom has been forgotten. Civil freedom has *not* been forgotten. Indeed, it is highly valued and protected. But not economic freedom; very few these days have even heard of it. It has been forgotten because it does not exist in practice in the current time; at least not commonly, perhaps only in isolated pockets of the world, where native peoples exist living under native rule. The vast majority of people in the world today do not live under economic freedom; they do not *experience* economic freedom. Hence, the two aspects to life in a community – civil and economic – are not equally strong. Community life is "lopsided".

Civil freedom allows for the fulfilment of civil life, and to protect civil freedom we have *law* – law that we all agree to live by. Deviations from civil law – assault and theft, for example – we simply will not tolerate. As a people we will not tolerate abuse in the civil realm. Man-made law acts as a restraint upon those actions that would spoil or destroy civil freedom.

Civil freedom consists in four particular expressions of freedom: freedom of person, freedom of speech, freedom of movement and freedom of association. It is protection from assault and from theft of one's property, the freedom to say what one wishes to say (except it be defamatory), the freedom to go where one wishes to go when one wishes to go, and the freedom to meet with whomsoever one wishes to meet. Such is the high level of civil freedom we live under and enjoy that it tends to be taken for granted. We do not consciously notice it. The value of civil freedom does become obvious, though, if that freedom is threatened. The 2011 riots in the city of London were a painful reminder of this.

After having lived under civil freedom it is difficult to imagine living any other way. Precisely the same would be said of *economic* freedom if people had actually experienced it: it would be difficult to imagine living any other way!

The root meaning of the word *freedom* is dear, beloved, beautiful, joyful (from the root "free" and the Sanskrit "priya"); and support, nourishment (from the root "dom"). Thus, freedom supports, upholds, nourishes, and is dear to people's hearts. One way of describing freedom is that it is the law of friends (Mason, 2007). This is a beautiful description, and points clearly toward what economic freedom is about.

Freedom is prosperity: prosperity not necessarily in the sense of the accumulation of physical wealth, but the prosperity of *good living,* including having sufficient food, adequate shelter, good company, a sense of being useful, and goodwill – the last foundation of freedom. Another description of freedom is "to be set free from the strictures of necessity" (MacLaren 1943, p. 162).

Economic freedom is the reign of equity, the reign of justice. Economic freedom is the natural state for a community to live in. There are strong moves by people to seek economic freedom, even though they may not ever have heard of it. The search for freedom is strong.

When considering what freedom means, the question that naturally arises is, freedom from what? The answer is that it depends on the circumstances. For some, freedom will mean release from gaol, for others it will mean something quite different. But people do seek freedom! There is a strong *notion* of freedom in the human being, and a strong desire that freedom may prevail.

Economic freedom is very much a matter of the heart. This is why it is so important. It is at the very heart of economic life. Of course, economic freedom *does* have its physical manifestations (expressed as *good living*) but its essence is of the heart. People *feel* freedom, or its absence. Living in freedom is not the outcome of an intellectual decision. And it is deeper than appearances. An *appearance* of freedom is akin to an appearance of being happy: look beneath the surface and an apparently happy individual may not be happy at all. And happiness, like economic freedom, is not an intellectual state. Someone is happy or they are not. It is a state of *being,* not a state of thinking. Likewise, economic freedom is a state of being. A man or woman living under conditions of real economic freedom will *feel* free with regard to matters economic, and his or her behaviour will reflect this spirit of freedom. There will be total independence with respect to economic matters – for example, certainly no fear of "how will I meet my mortgage repayment?" – and there will be the experience of creativity and enthusiasm.

Whilst first impressions may be that we do have economic freedom (and a few *do* have it because they can "do what they like" in all respects economically) the following several observations are clear indication that, as a people, as a community, we do not.

- Many are homeless and live only by virtue of the aid of charity
- There exist many monotonous occupations (including those in high-technology industries), engagement in which demonstrably "dulls the human spirit"
- The bottom quartile of wage earners struggle to "make ends meet" financially
- Social unrest over unfavourable or unacceptable economic conditions is commonplace

Attempts by people at *securing* economic freedom, or at least some degree of it, are currently made by way of:

- increasingly advanced levels of higher education (so that the graduate can get a "better" job – better than his or her neighbour)
- investment activity – property and share ownership
- a proliferation of small businesses (coffee shops, retail clothing/shoes shops)
- farming (farmers "buy" their economic freedom via buying and owning their land)

However, all of the above only give economic freedom to those who can successfully pursue these avenues – many cannot – and so it is not economic freedom *for everyone*. And it is not the *real* economic freedom because each of the above "opportunities" exacts its own price! Each of them has to be *purchased*. The real economic freedom is free. If it is not so it is not freedom. Economic freedom is not purchased. It is mankind's birthright.

Exactly as is the situation for civil freedom, for economic freedom to prevail there has to be appropriate man-made law. But we don't have it! Our tolerance of abuse in the realm of economic life is incredible! – Stupid, really. It is in the realm of the unbelievable that as civilised people we tolerate such gross and glaring abuses of natural justice! Unfortunately, examples of this abuse are many and insidious. They include:

- company executives being paid multi-million dollar salaries and then serious university research being conducted to find out the "ethics" of this
- half our nearest Asian neighbour's population of 220 million people living in abject poverty whilst foreigners (including Australians) are "called in" and paid as consultants, or to complete PhDs, into the cause of poverty there when the cause is staring any even half-awake person in the face
- Australia conducting (another!) review of homelessness in this country when even the blind and the dumb know the cause of the problem
- 3 billion people of the world living on less than $2 per day
- 24,000 people *dying* every day from starvation

All of these examples are unfortunate demonstrations of the absence of economic freedom, and examples, therefore, of injustice: injustice after injustice after injustice! And if these examples are not enough, right in the midst of western wealth and affluence some 46 million US citizens used "food stamps" during May of 2011; and approximately 80 per cent of families in Australia with children younger than fifteen years of age received Family Tax Benefits during the 2009/10 year. Over the course of a year these benefits help about seven million people (parents and children), or roughly one-third of the population. There are more than 800,000 Australians in receipt of the Disability Support Pension – about 5 per cent of all Australians of working age; and more than half a million in receipt of unemployment benefits. All this is "cause for deep national shame" (*The Australian,* 23 December 2010, pp. 1, 4).

It is obvious, surely, that for the fulfilment of economic life, proper *economic* law is necessary. And surely it is equally obvious that proper economic law is now absent.

The effect on the subject, economics, of economic freedom having been forgotten

Because economic freedom has been forgotten the subject, economics, has gone astray.

> The economics profession continues to present a poor, incoherent, and frankly inadequate face to the wider society, one of whose key facets it purports to understand. Either it does. Or it doesn't. It is time to confront the possibility of failure and withdraw to sort out the mess (Radford 2011).

A belief in and adherence to economic freedom as the natural and expected state under which civilised people live would give economics *direction.* It would be the guiding star for economics. But economic freedom is not recognised now, not known about. Henry George *did* know about it, and so in 1879 said:

> ... Properly understood, the laws which govern the production and distribution of wealth show that the want and injustice of the present social system are not necessary; but that on the contrary a social state is possible in which poverty would be unknown, and **all the better qualities and higher powers of human nature would have opportunity**

for full development (George [1879] 1992, pp. 559-560 (author's emphasis)).

With regard to "the laws which govern the production and distribution of wealth", John Paul II said: "They (market forces) could play their beneficial role only when they functioned under individuals who are free" (Kwitney 1997, p. 337).

Economics and law are intimately related. Indeed, it might be said that economics *is* law – that law relating to the economic aspect of life. Law formulated under the knowledge of economic freedom would have the effect of allowing the people whom it is meant to serve to actually live under economic freedom. And economic freedom would be the guiding star for the formulation of economic law. In 2007 a London-based lawyer and philosopher, and keen advocate for justice, Ian Mason, gave a lecture on jurisprudence, which he describes as including justice and being the philosophy of law. Mason says that the basis of jurisprudence is that we live in a lawful universe; that the law is already given. This given law he refers to as "wild law". It is embodied in the existence and workings of the universe. It is not human law, not man-made law, but law that exists already. To *discover* what this "given" law is, the question that needs to be asked is: What is natural to the human being? He suggests the following are natural:

- Freedom
- Love
- The ability to develop and grow in knowledge
- Happiness

Wild law

Notice that first on the list is *freedom,* and so the purpose of law (and therefore economics) is to have people live in freedom; which, believes Ian Mason, will, in turn, *bring out the best in human life.* Further, he suggests that the basic and natural understanding with respect to law is that everything should flourish. Law should allow things to flourish. Wild law *does* allow things to flourish.

In addition to its one great function of allowing for economic freedom, wild law has other, related applications. Examples of these applications are genetic engineering, control over the use of land, and corporate behaviour. With respect to genetic engineering, wild law dictates that nature should not be fiddled with. In practice, this means that if you are going to fiddle with nature – such as genetically modifying crops – it must be *demonstrably safe to proceed,* with the onus of demonstration on the one who wants to fiddle. With respect to land use, controls can be introduced – even though freehold title means you can do with your land what you like. Planning regulations do just that: control the use to which land can be put. With respect to corporate behaviour, corporates could – should – be *restrained* in their commercial behaviour to consider "proper livelihoods" for their employees and to be persuaded that the existence of the corporation *not* be solely to provide profits for those who do not work in it (i.e. shareholders). Wild law – law that is at the heart of the natural universe – is at the very foundation of economic freedom.

The well-known American transcendental philosopher, Ralph Waldo Emerson, had an almost-equally well-known companion, Henry David Thoreau, and Thoreau spoke of the life of a wise man or woman. He said:

> To be a philosopher is not merely to have subtle thoughts, nor even to found a school, but so to love wisdom as to live according to its dictates, a life of simplicity, independence, magnanimity, and trust. It is to solve some of the problems of life, not only theoretically, but practically.

Thoreau, himself, loved independence. That is to say, he loved freedom. He valued it highly. He believed (and *lived*) that everyone should value it highly. And the *first* problem to be solved, in his view, was that of getting a living. "Getting a living is the most practically important of all questions because everyone must answer it before going on to explore and then express the possibilities of freedom" (Thoreau [1906] 1951, p. 164).

The essence of economic freedom is *independence*. Economic independence is not meant in the sense of "having a lot of money and therefore not having to work", but in the sense of having the opportunity, the option, of being able to work and earn a living *without having to come to terms with another party* – in particular, an employer or a landlord. Under economic freedom the opportunity exists, for anyone who so wishes, to make or earn a living in total and absolute independence of the favour of or acceptance by anybody else. Under freedom, in the act of earning a living the individual is either perfectly content to be an employee and work under the direction of an employer, or has the readily-available opportunity to be dependent upon no one but himself. He may *co-operate* with others in his work – yes; *work* with others – yes; but *depend* upon someone else for his livelihood: no! *The man is his own master.*

To live in a state of independence is to live with at least a measure of prosperity. Economic freedom and poverty are not bedfellows. Except for religious and other ascetics[20] poverty is a strange state, utterly unnatural, unwelcome, not sought out. Under conditions of economic freedom, poverty is an impossibility. Poverty, deprivation – particularly *alongside* of others living in luxury and extravagance – is a state enforced upon people. Economics is the science of *prosperity,* and prosperity has no business with deprivation.

Men and women living in communities under the blessed, natural state of economic freedom have the option to live, move and work at their own will, at their own discretion, not necessarily according to the mind-set of an employer who has interests and priorities utterly different

---

[20] But the life of these people would in no way be described as "poor" by any who understands what religious ascetics are about. Indeed, their life is very *full.*

from one's own. Economic freedom is being able to give full, free and unhindered expression to the talents and abilities within the human being, and to enjoy the full fruits thereof. Economic freedom is complete *fulfilment* in the economic sense.

Why economic freedom does *not* prevail

At the first-principles level of a discussion upon this question, the most significant of the reasons that economic freedom does not prevail is that the individual who wants to work usually has to come to terms with someone else – an employer or a landlord – regarding the conditions under which he or she may have access to the natural resources necessary to work: in particular, access to a work space (or site). Such having to come to terms implies dependence, and dependence is the negation of freedom. For the individual living under economic freedom there is total self-reliance, there is no one with whom he or she necessarily has to come to terms in order to work.

Of course it is pertinent to note that not everyone will want to work independently, by themselves. Not everyone will want to be their own master. Many people – perhaps the majority – will be content to work for an employer of some kind or another, will be content to work on terms dictated by another. But not everyone. And for economic freedom to reign, the practical possibility of going to work entirely independently *needs to exist,* even if only a few avail themselves of the opportunity. Economic freedom is when conditions exist to allow for independent work, even though few may take up the opportunity. The important point is that the many who do not take it up need to know that it *is available,* that they do have an *option.*

Being able to work for oneself and at one's own discretion is not necessarily going to lead to a trouble-free life. There may well be mistakes, failures, hardships, that would have been avoided if the person concerned had worked under direction – had worked for an employer. But, mistakes and hardships notwithstanding, the outcome of living independently will be a strong, free, vigorous spirit; and anyhow, no matter what the arguments for and against, living entirely independently simply may be what that person *wants!*

What is required for economic freedom to prevail?

The essential requirement for economic freedom to reign is free, unhindered access to the natural resources that are necessary for work to take place. A simple way of viewing economic freedom is to consider what would happen if everyone owned at least that amount of land that was required for them to conduct their work on. It is not *necessary* to economic freedom that this should be so, but it is useful to consider the *implications* of workers owning the site upon which they do or may work. For a farmer growing wheat in Australia this would mean owning many hundreds of acres, for a computer technician just enough square feet to house a work bench and the required tools of trade, for a retailer a shop of sufficient size to display the stock. If each owned his or her work site, then plainly all could simply go to work on that site, without having first to make arrangements or come to terms with someone else in order to obtain a site.

There is, indeed, a body of informed, intelligent opinion which argues that, for freedom and independence to reign, there must be a restoration of private property. Hilaire Belloc ([1936] 2002, p. 27) says: "It has been found in practice, and the truth is witnessed to by the instincts in all of us, that widely distributed property as a condition of freedom is necessary to the normal satisfaction of human nature". William Somerset Maugham ([1944] 2000) revealed an understanding of the strong sense of the desire to own property and the effect of ownership when he wrote, " ... When she told him that year by year she was buying a bit of land in her native village, he felt a thrill of pride. He knew the desire to own land that is in the heart of every person ... " (p. 190). Leon MacLaren (1993) said, not so very long ago after a period of overseas travel: "I'll tell you what I noticed as I went around the world: I noticed that the peoples of different countries were divided very simply. Those who had land were of one kind, and those who had not got land were of another, and there was the class distinction, bold and clear" (pp. 199-200). Andrew MacLaren (father of Leon), the British member of parliament from 1922 to 1945, regularly spoke out in The House of Commons, *God gave the land to the people; then why haven't they got it?*" MacLaren's "hero" was Campbell-Bannerman, whose oft-repeated pledge was "to make the land less of a pleasure ground for the rich, and more of a treasure-house for the nation". Of course, mankind cannot live without access to land, and so if people do not have this access then they will simply *take* it! They have to! – Because life without land is impossible. An unfortunate example of this is evident in the life of the homeless who live on park benches or in other public places – obviously all sited on land, all of them sites which the unfortunate homeless *take* access of (temporary though that access be).

Ownership of landed property[21] by all members of the working population is not necessary for economic freedom to prevail. But certainly it would be a step in the *direction* of economic freedom. It would grant the owner at least some measure of freedom. Ownership of one's house and enough land to run a chosen business on would certainly ensure a degree of economic freedom – quite a high degree, in fact. However, the real economic freedom means freedom for *everyone*, not just some property-owning sub-set of the population. Individual private property – by definition – excludes the common interest, and excludes those who do not own property.

---

[21] It is of interest to note that rural shires in Australia used to insist on ownership of landed property as a necessary condition for being able to vote. Right up until relatively recently (the 1950s /60s), only **ratepayers** (i.e. those who paid rates on privately-owned property) were eligible to vote in local government elections. This is because the right to vote was (quite rightly) taken as a privilege, to be used responsibly, and that ownership of property was seen as indicating the presence of a level of responsibility appropriate to a voter being given the right to participate in government.

Economic freedom does not prevail in modern-day economies, but strong intimations of it existed in earlier times. People living in England prior to the eighteenth century had free and ready access to common land ("the commons"), and thus *felt, experienced,* a sense of economic freedom. When the common lands were taken away from them – which period coincided with the "industrial revolution" – there were violent mass protests. The people felt they were losing their freedom – indeed they were losing their freedom – and protested vehemently and violently against this loss. Historians generally attribute this great protest movement to the mechanisation of industry. The real reason for the protests, though, was the loss of freedom – freedom to make use of the common lands.

Free access to natural resources – the fundamental requirement for economic freedom to prevail – means that free land must be available. This does *not* mean that *all* land will be or needs to be free; rather, that land *at the margin* is free. Land "at the margin" is that land or site that benefits least from the presence of community, and so it is that land that would be sought after least of all by would-be occupants (and not sought after at all by occupants of better sites).

Steps toward economic freedom

Over recent years and in the course of history there have been specific practical steps taken in the direction of securing economic freedom. Although economic freedom has not prevailed commonly, these steps, "economic policies" in contemporary language, were in the right direction. They include:

1. Site-value land taxation: which, amongst other things, removes the possibility of land being a plaything of investors. Landlordism is the mechanism that allows the fruit of work to be transferred from those who do the work to those who own (control) the land

2. Death duties:[22] which duties have the effect of re-distributing concentrations of wealth after the recipient of such wealth has died

3. The current Canberra land rental scheme: whereby intending home-owners do not buy, but rent from local government the land upon which they build their house, thus avoiding the crippling effect of mortgage payments upon what otherwise would be very expensive land. Under the land rental scheme, mortgage repayments by home owners are in the order of *one half* of what they would be had the land been purchased in the "normal" way

4. The jubilee-year redistribution of wealth: a fundamental redistribution of property every fifty years, as set out in the Book of Leviticus, chapter 25

Although economic freedom does not exist these days, there are *reflections* of it in practice, faint though these reflections may be. *Farmers* work under a kind of economic freedom, made possible by the fact that they *buy* the land they farm on. In effect, they are purchasing their economic freedom. The fact that they own their land, and therefore can do with it what they like and when they like, allows them to work independently, a trait that farmers are renowned for. The outcome of working in this way is hardy, vigorous souls, productive, adaptive and innovative. However, not every one who would like to farm can afford the capital sum involved to buy the necessary land, and so only relatively few have the opportunity of this form of "economic freedom". Another example of a taste of economic freedom is that of the many people who have been fortunate enough to get a good formal education and then work in careers of their own choosing and interest, for very satisfactory monetary reward. A further example of a faint reflection of economic freedom is the traditional Australian practice of ownership of one's own house and "quarter-acre"

---

[22] It is pertinent to consider the use of the word, *duties*, in this context. Its specific use implies that the originator of the name, 'death duties' – and probably many others – believed that the payment of this money ("death duty") was the *duty* of the one who had died, that it was *due* – due to be paid to his or her fellow human beings (i.e. the community).

block of land. Even though this land may not be the place of work, it is a place where the occupants can "do what they like", and so experience a taste of economic freedom. Further, it *is* the place of work for some; hence, again, there will be a taste of freedom. So, economic freedom is not entirely unknown in this country. That is part[23] of the reason thousands – millions – of people from other lands would like to come and live here.

These are examples of weak reflections of economic freedom, but an important point to note in having cited them is that they are only *partial*. All of them are only partial because, first, they offer only a taste of full economic freedom; and second, because only a part of the population enjoys these tastes of freedom, and so the community as a whole does not experience it. For the real economic freedom to prevail, freedom must be available to everyone. Economic freedom that is available only to *some* is not really economic freedom at all. Its scope must include not only the "privileged", nor just the "underprivileged", but everyone – the strong, the weak, the intelligent, the dull, the honest and the "average". *Everybody* wants to be free. A former prime minister, Malcolm Fraser (2010), said that "he believed in small government because he believed in freedom – individual freedom" (p. 349).

In summary, what is needed for economic freedom to prevail is:

(i)   free access to a work site – a "marginal" site, one that nobody else currently occupies (access to other, more productive sites, will *not* be free)
(ii) full and free choice of occupation
(iii) total dependence and reliance upon oneself for one's livelihood

The natural order of the very basis of economic activity involves a two-fold coincidence: human needs, and the ability to meet those needs. Ability to meet those needs is, in turn, a two-fold matter: the desire, intelligence and energy of the human being, and ready access to the natural resources that are to be shaped into useful end products.

---

[23] The other part, of course, is the strong environment of *civil* freedom here.

Economic freedom is the existence of the unhindered and independent ability to allow the full expression of the natural desire to be employed in making a living. It is the engagement in economic life entirely as a matter of free will.

What happens in the absence of economic freedom?

Where engagement with the world is *not* of one's free will – that is to say, where engagement takes place in the absence of economic freedom – there will be, in varying degrees, resentment, resistance, withdrawal, anti-social behaviour, and *the seeking of alternatives* (such as drugs) in an attempt to find human satisfaction. Manifestations of the absence of economic freedom include:

1. Poverty (in all its forms – including homelessness)
2. Job dissatisfaction, restlessness in employment (particularly amongst the young)
3. Proliferation of "leisure" activities – in particular, an emphasis on sport as a means of seeking satisfaction
4. Proliferation of certain small businesses, such as coffee shops – attempts by people to "have a go" at being their own master
5. A stampede of desire for higher academic qualifications (and the consequent deterioration of university standards) – fierce competition for places at the better universities
6. All manner of *social* unrest (violence and family break-ups in particular)

Perhaps the most pervasive and harmful of the outcomes of an absence of economic freedom is that people, who are inherently good, become selfish.

People are only mean when they're threatened. And that's what our culture does. That's what our economy does. Even people who have jobs in our economy are threatened, because they worry about losing them. And when you get threatened, you start looking out only for yourself. You start making money a god" (Albom 1997, p. 154).

This view, that people become selfish only when threatened, certainly explains very much of the darker side of the present rundown in economic social behaviour.

What happens in the *presence* of economic freedom?

In the presence of economic freedom, engagement with the world is a matter of free will. Life is enhanced and fulfilled thereby. The fruits of the rule of economic freedom may be considered from two perspectives: the opportunity to be one's own master, and full and free choice of occupation.

1. Economic freedom ensures the opportunity to be one's own master, which opportunity encourages, indeed ensures, the taking of *personal responsibility* and the experience, in full, of doing so. Emerson ([1841] 1982), in his essay, "Self Reliance", emphasises the importance of taking responsibility.
2. Economic freedom ensures full and free choice of occupation, which greatly assists in a sense of fulfilment and the use and development of natural talents.

The use and development of natural talents is a source of happiness to the individual, and a benefit to all other members of the community. Simple examples include the practice and refinement of delicate heart and brain surgery – plainly perfected by those following the path of their own choosing; and the magnificent photographic works of Melbourne photography icon, John Street. Notice how *everyone,* not just the individual innovators concerned, benefits from these developments and refinements. Economic freedom stimulates, encourages, allows for, calls forth the development and expression of talents, the opportunity to speak, and the development of responsibility.

One of the practical and obvious manifestations of economic freedom is full employment. With the exception of the young, the old, the sick and those engaged in the full-time care of homes and children, everyone will be employed when economic freedom reigns. This is a natural state of affairs. Everyone will be employed because they need to be productive (in order to provide for themselves and their natural dependants) and because they want to be productive – the natural desire to work. The provision and ready-availability of a free work site (at the margin) ensures that nobody is not productively employed. Those who, for whatever reason, cannot come to terms with an employer, nor can arrange business affairs to be able to finance and manage the renting of a site and the other necessary arrangements involved in being self-employed on a better site, will take up work on the free site.

The availability of land free of charge is not an idea of fantasy, nor is it an act of extreme socialism. It is a fact of nature. *All* sites are, in fact, provided by nature free of charge. A rental charge arises in the ordinary course of economic affairs as a means of allocating sites amongst competing occupants. *All* sites are not, and will not, be required for use. It is an observable fact that not all land is in use; there is always some unused land in existence. Unused sites have no natural rental value. This is because nobody wants them for use. (This is obvious: it is why they are vacant). Hence, to make unused sites – sites at the margin – available free of charge to those few who will need them is an action designed both to meet a need and be in accordance with the natural order of things. Paul Johnson (1997) certainly believed so. In his view, free land was a vital factor in the extraordinary growth of wealth in America.

The basic economic fact about the New World was that land was plentiful ... To get immigrants you had to offer them land, and once they arrived they were determined to become individual entrepreneurs, subject to no one but the law. In North America, the settlement and actual ownership of land came first. What flag you lived under was secondary – it was successful farming and ownership of land which brought you personal independence, the only kind which really mattered (pp. 61-62).

The provision of free sites at the margin is an important, though ordinary action, not a hare-brained idea. It always has been important in the historical economic development of nations; it always will be important.

The following statements of social and political leaders reveal an innate understanding by them of the importance of economic freedom. Former Liberal politician, John Hewson said:

... The lesson of towns like Inglewood is that bad times pass provided the people who live through them never lose faith in themselves and hope in the future ...

... The people who built this country had big dreams and if many of them failed, we are much the better for their efforts. I suspect that worries about occupational health, job security, leave loadings and lump sums never entered the heads of the men and women who tamed the bush, worked the mines and built this town. If they had wanted security they would never have left London or Melbourne. Caution would never have built this town. Timidity would never have developed this country. Conservatism would never have made Australia prosper. If our distant past shows that hardship can build a nation, more recent experience shows that comfort produces a society of under-achievers. The challenge for our generation is to recover a pioneering spirit while remaining a generous society (Abjorensen 1993, p. 198).

Ronald Reagan, speaking of how the American growth miracle was created and of man's innate drive to be free, said:

No matter what your background, no matter how lowly your station in life, there must be no limit on your ability to reach for the stars, to go as far as your God-given talents will take you. Trust the people; believe every human being is capable of greatness, capable of self-government ... Only when people are free to worship, create, and build, only when they are given a personal stake in deciding their destiny and benefiting from their own risks, only then do societies become dynamic, prosperous, progressive, and free.

... Time was on the side of the democracies. All over the world there were indications that democracy was on the rise and Communism was near collapse, dying from a terminal disease called tyranny. It could no longer bottle up the energy of the human spirit and man's innate drive to be free (Reagan 1990, pp. 476, 555).

John Grey Gorton, speaking from the office of Australian Prime Minister, 1968, also had an eye toward freedom. He said:

I would like to see ... a nation of intense technological and scientific achievement. A nation in which no one who is worth anything is unemployed and in which there is an opportunity for every man and woman to be employed in that field of endeavour to which they are drawn. A nation in which there is no poverty and in which the fear of age, illness and invalidism is removed ... We are on the road to all these things ... (Trengove 1969, p. 13).

And Adam Smith knew about freedom:

The natural effort of every individual to better his own condition, when suffered to exert itself with freedom and security, is so powerful a principle, that it is alone, and without any assistance, not only capable of carrying on the society to wealth and prosperity, but of surmounting a hundred impertinent obstructions with which the folly of human laws too often encumbers its operations (Landes 1999, p. 219).

So, whilst economic freedom is scarcely heard of these days and is not so much as mentioned in any of the mainstream economics courses offered by Australia's universities, there exists among people a strong sense of freedom and a strong desire to have it. Tom Mann, an acquaintance of Henry George, believed that they *would* have it. Of the economics of George's *Progress and Poverty* Mann wrote:

> ... a fine stimulus to me, full of incentive to noble endeavour, throwing light on many questions of real importance, and giving me a glorious hope for the future of humanity, a firm conviction that the social problem could and would be solved ... Never since I gave it careful attention have I had one hour of doubt but that the destiny of the human race is assured, and that those who work will, in due time, come to occupy their rightful position (Mann 1979, p. 39).

Henry George and economic freedom

To the extent that he is known at all, Henry George is known today as the proponent of the "single tax" (a tax on land rents). But Henry George was really interested in *freedom* – freedom for the peoples of the world and particularly for those living in economic bondage. He knew what freedom meant and it was this knowledge, and the energy that came with it, that had him write *Progress and Poverty* and then tour the western world giving lectures on human progress and what was needed to allow for, and to encourage, its flowering. His real interest was not taxation at all. Taxation, for its own sake, was not what his great work was about. The land tax was simply the *means* for freeing up natural resources for use (land in particular) and thereby creating the physical conditions that would allow people – all people – to work in freedom. He spoke of the land tax because of the effect that it has on the availability of land. Land being free makes the human being free, because access to land is mankind's primary (first!) need. And so it is *freedom* that Henry George was about: economic freedom for mankind. *This* is what made him such a great man. *This* is why more copies of *Progress and Poverty* were sold in its time than any other book except the Bible.

And so in summary, what is needed for economic freedom to prevail is to *remove the possibility of land being an investment good.* What is needed is *not* that land be unavailable for private ownership and use, but that it be rendered unavailable as an investment good. A large part of the demand for land currently comes from those seeking *investment* in property. Because of the special nature of land (see chapter 4), and because rise in its price presents an investor with unearned income – *unjust* income (see chapter 6) – land should be protected from such activity. Such protection is important. The desire to own land appears to be innate in the human being and very strong. Respected historian and described by some as "one of the greatest friends of sanity", Hilaire Belloc commented upon the propensity and ramifications of the instinct to own property:

> ... widely distributed property as a condition of freedom is necessary to the normal satisfaction of human nature. In the absence of widely distributed property, general culture ultimately fails and so certainly does citizenship. The cells of the body politic are atrophied and the mass of men have not even, at last, an opinion of their own, but are moulded by the few who retain ownership of land and endowments and reserves. So property is essential to a full life ... (Belloc [1936] 2002, pp. 27-28).

In Belloc's view, not only is property necessary to the satisfaction of human nature: its absence leads to the ultimate failure of culture! But it is necessary for its *use* value, not as part of an investment portfolio.

Economic freedom and the land tax

Protection of land from the ravages of investors is effected by the levying of a land resource rental tax, with the tax collecting the full site rental value of the land. This simple, but powerful action would have a profound effect on the demand for land – freeing it up to be available for those who want to use it. And this, in turn, would have a profound effect on the price of land. In particular, it would have a major effect on the affordability of a home, and on the ability to own and run a business. The remedy for the absence of economic freedom is simple; but as has been said already, the truth is always simple, justice is simple: render unto Caesar the things that are Caesar's and unto God the things that are God's.

Henry George knew what freedom was. He said,

> It is not enough that the people should be theoretically equal before the law. They must have liberty to avail themselves of the opportunities and means of life; they must stand on equal terms, with reference to the bounty of nature. Either this, or liberty withdraws her light! (quoted in Stewart 2008, p. 185).

And Henry George knew the importance of access to land for economic freedom to prevail. John Steinbeck (1939) knew what freedom was. So did *Shankaracharya* (2003), occupant of one of India's four traditional seats of wisdom.

> If a nation values anything more than freedom, it will lose its freedom; and the irony of it is that if it is comfort or money that it values more, it will lose that too ... Essence of humanity is fulfilment of the law ... The essence of the law is the prosperity or well-being of the people. Apart from prosperity there is the absolute function of the law, the freedom, total freedom (Shankaracharya, *Tradition* booklet, 16 April 2003).

Economic freedom is really about allowing for, making provision for, the full expression of the different natures of human beings. Some naturally flourish on being closely directed employees, whilst others inwardly "revolt" at this prospect and insist on working for themselves and being entirely under their own direction. Either way, what is important is the happiness and well-being of the individual, because, apart from these two being desirable in their own right, their presence fosters and encourages the drawing out of hidden talents and living a fulfilling life. An intelligent man or woman working on a repetitive assembly line, for example, has hardly anything drawn out of him during such a working life, and so a most important part of his life is a waste.

Freedom, total freedom, is the natural condition for humankind. Economic freedom is the rule under which people are left to find their place in life quite naturally; and economics is meant to be the knowledge that makes the way clear for men and women *to* find their place in life quite naturally. Economics, properly understood, is the elevating, noble knowledge which, through its application, allows people living in communities to go about their daily lives of providing for themselves and their dependants without fear of unemployment, without fear of poverty, in a spirit of freedom, and working in an occupation through which their natural skills and talents will be drawn forth and given full expression.

Chapter 10

Immediate Matters

We put our values in the wrong things. And it leads to very disillusioned lives. I think we should talk about that.

Mitch Albom

Injustice and economic bondage[24] are the two great plights suffered by large numbers of the world's population. The prevalence of injustice is horrific, and there are few that escape its effects. A majority of observers would probably agree that poverty is the most obvious economic problem facing the world today, particularly the extreme, debilitating forms of it that may be seen on our television screens every day.

> Slum poverty is unacceptable ... It is time democracy catered for all, and not only for the greatest number. It is time to stop, instead of passing by on the other side. Handouts are the usual social democratic answer, but they are temporary and breed dependence. Respect holds the key (Stewart 2008, p. 176).

There is a dreadful irony in the very existence of extreme poverty in the world. First, properly considered, economics is the study of

---

[24] The *absence* of economic freedom.

abundance. The real interest of good economics is in prosperity. It is the study of how all may benefit from and enjoy abundance – which *would* be the situation if justice ruled. As has been noted already, the world *as a whole* is not poor – in fact, it is very wealthy. Significant economic goals that were set over fifty years ago have been achieved many times over. Since the establishment of the Bretton Woods agreement[25] in 1944, the world has seen a twelve-fold increase in global trade and a five-fold increase in economic growth. It (the Bretton Woods agreement) gave the West "25 years of stability and unprecedented growth both in international trade and in domestic material prosperity ... and the longest period of financial stability in history" (Teese 2012, p. 9). Second, economics promised so much.

> Nineteenth-century economists predicted that the abundance made possible by technological advance and the modern organisation of work would result in the emergence of 'post-materialist' humans – people existing on a higher plane, where their cultural, intellectual and spiritual powers are refined ... The 1960s and 1970s saw a flood of literature predicting a future in which technological progress would allow for us to work only a few hours a week and our main problem would be how best to enjoy our leisure (Hamilton and Denniss 2005, pp. 4-5).

But these promises have not materialised and, instead, the bitter fruits of injustice are clearly on display. A billion people go hungry on a planet with sufficient food for all – Australians alone threw away more then $5.2 billion worth of food and drink in 2004[26] – while another billion put their

---

[25] The Bretton Woods agreement, concluded under the guidance of the United States and Britain, was an agreement on an international monetary system for the world's major industrial states, established July 1944 at a conference of forty-four Allied nations in Bretton Woods, New Hampshire, the United States. The impetus for the agreement came out of the economic horrors of the Great Depression. The agreement officially ceased August 1971 when the US unilaterally terminated convertibility of the dollar to gold. The agreement was based on the idea of the US dollar as the basic international trading currency, underwritten by the US government – a *de facto* gold standard with a number of built-in stabilisers.

[26] Hamilton and Denniss 2005, p. 103.

health at risk by eating too much![27] And poverty is not the only problem. Large numbers, very large numbers, of people are unemployed; whilst the richest one per cent of the world's population have so much money that all they can do with most of it is buy real estate and thereby push up its price, thus making life harder for those who need land simply to live on and work on.

This is the unfortunate story of injustice, and as for economic freedom: that is all but a dream, even for those few who have heard of it! Daily economic life is commonly experienced as a scramble for survival, not the uplifting and elevating experience it is meant to be and *would* be in the presence of economic freedom. And all of this economic misery is happening in a time when formal economic knowledge has never been greater. What a mess! Little wonder that Allan Bloom (1987) said, "higher education has failed democracy and impoverished the souls of today's students"; and that Mueller (2010) says, "Economics is primed for – and in desperate need of – a revolution ... The myopic focus of modern economics leads us astray". Yet Henry George knew the solution well when he wrote all those years ago in 1879, and no fewer than five British Prime Ministers (including Winston Churchill) agreed with him; Singapore and Hong Kong have thrived on the adoption of his economic wisdom – the practical application of which is a land tax; and the Henry Review (2010; *Recommendations 1 and 52*), recommends a broad-based land tax on grounds of efficiency benefits. And a land tax was enshrined in the policy platform of Australia's oldest political party.[28]

The essence of economic freedom is that each man is his own master. That is to say, he lives in complete independence, economically – he depends upon nobody else in the matter of making a living. The desire for freedom is strong, and manifests itself plainly. Archbishop Desmond Tutu was critically aware of the importance of freedom for his people and

---

[27] Melbourne *Age*, 21 January 2012, p. 20.

[28] In an act of gross ignorance, the land tax was removed only relatively recently from that policy platform.

the place of land in that freedom when he reportedly said (though no doubt with at least the hint of a twinkle in his eye): "Before the Europeans came to Africa, we had the land and they had the Bible. We bowed our heads to pray, and when we opened our eyes, we had the Bible and they had the land". The great rise of the American people is a direct result of a high degree of economic freedom that was available to them in the early centuries of the settling and development of that nation. Land was readily available – free to begin with – and relatively cheap for a long time afterward, and new arrivals made the most of this opportunity of being able to gain access to affordable land, the very opportunity that was denied them in Europe. Speaking of eighteenth-century America, Paul Johnson (1997) writes: " ... For the first time in human history, cheap, good land was available to the multitude. This happy prospect was now open, and it remained so for the best part of the next two centuries; then it closed, for ever" (p. 86). The same was the case in Australia during the early years of her settlement and development, and the outcome, likewise, was a community of free and hardy souls.[29]

But all this has changed. Land is now expensive, prohibitively expensive to most of those younger people who want to become farmers, and, perhaps even more importantly, to many who need to buy a home. One of the consequences of this situation is that there is an over-abundance of small business start-ups by hopeful entrepreneurs who would like to be their own master – food outlets, shoe shops, coffee shops, retail clothing outlets. Many fail, or last for only a short time; but the prospect of being able to be one's own master is deeply alluring, and so there are plenty of candidates to take the place of those who fail. But the depressing pattern of enthusiastic, idealistic, would-be entrepreneurs very soon becoming

---

[29] Changing, though, now. The land of free and hardy souls is fast becoming a place of dependency, irresponsibility, bureaucratic domination, selfishness, extremes, and the place where, surrounded by people (mainly lawyers and accountants) who are forever saying "it can't be done", it is increasingly difficult to get anything done – except for the passing of ever-more restrictive laws and the calling of "enquiries" and the study of their petty, dead, defunct "findings".

disillusioned, financially-poorer, failed small businesspersons, continues. And it is all so predictable! Yet the viable, natural, alternative is available – but not availed! How different was the situation in the early years of America's development. Again speaking of the eighteenth century:

> ... everything was working in America's favour. The rate of expansion was about 40 per cent or even more each decade. The availability of land meant large family units, rarely less than 60 acres, often well over 100, huge by European standards. Couples could marry earlier ... Living standards were high ... any male who survived to be forty could expect to live in a household of median income and capital wealth ... The shortage of labour meant artisans did not need to form guilds to protect jobs. It was rare to find restrictions on entry to any trade. Few skilled men remained hired employees beyond the age of twenty-five. If they did not acquire their own farm they ran their own business (Johnson 1997, pp. 94-95).

Seventeenth- and eighteenth-century America is the story of economic freedom – freedom made possible and practicable by virtue of the availability of a plentiful supply of "cheap and good" land. But how things have changed! The frustrating part of this whole pathetic story is that contemporary economists, most historians (and very nearly everybody else) seem totally unaware of the place and importance of land in all of this. When land is "cheap" and in good supply: prosperity reigns! When land is expensive, very expensive: strife and poverty prevail! Absence of economic freedom is costly. Economic bondage imposes a very high price.

But poverty, distressing though it is to observe (and undoubtedly much more distressing to live under) is a *symptom,* and to delve below the surface in order to seek out causes I want to suggest that the single-most important matter causing troublesome economic and social distress is a great "disconnectedness". There is widespread disconnection, or alienation, in whatever direction one looks. There is, for example, a hideous, morally-revolting disconnection between the value of the contribution and the size of the pay packet of the highest-paid corporate executives; and then more generally people are alienated from themselves, alienated from their neighbour, alienated from the larger community, alienated from their employer, alienated from nature itself. Even farmers, the "traditional custodians" of nature with a celebrated love of and relationship with her, are becoming disconnected from the soil by a cloud of chemicals. Chemical farming – the spraying of all manner of toxic chemicals upon soil and crops in order to attempt to control weeds and crop pests in the increasingly-difficult business of simply trying to make a living – has become common-place in almost all facets of agriculture, including cereal growing, dairy farming, vegetable production, rice growing and viticulture. Costs are rising, agricultural commodity prices are falling, and farmers are resorting to production techniques (the application of chemicals being one) they think will help them most to survive shrinking profit margins. Chemical farming also works toward production units (i.e. farms) becoming very much bigger, because it allows larger acreages to be worked and managed compared with what is possible using traditional mechanical farming methods. This, in turn, means heartache for the displaced farmers – those who are driven out in the mad rush by those who remain and "get big".

Away from farming and in the industrial sector, there are too many workplaces in which there is chronic disconnection between those working and that upon which they are working. Overly repetitive, monotonous work routines – motor car assembly lines, for example – have the effect of dulling the mind and senses of those who work at them, bringing about an almost total disconnection between human interest and intelligence and the actual job at hand; and the destruction of creativity and inventiveness. Further, disconnectedness breeds insecurity, and insecurity fosters greed. Loy makes specific note of the problem of greed, with the following: "Within economic theory and the market it promotes, the moral dimension of greed is inevitably lost (not taken into account); today it seems left to religion to preserve what is problematic about a human trait that is unsavoury at best and unambiguously evil at its worst" (David Loy, quoted in Mofid 2002, p. 47).

All of this was obvious to R.H. Tawney, and quite a long time ago:

> The most obvious facts are the most easily forgotten. Both the existing economic order and too many of the projects advanced for recon- structing it break down through their neglect of the truism that, since even quite common men have souls, no increase in material wealth will compensate them for arrangements which insult their self-respect and impair their freedom. A reasonable estimate of economic organi- sation must allow for the fact that, unless industry is to be paralysed by recurrent revolts on the part of outraged human nature, it must satisfy criteria which are not purely economic (*Religion and the Rise of Capitalism* (1926), quoted in Mofid 2002, p. v).

And "despite advances in material well-being we have not become happier in the process. Most of us have maximised our profits and incomes but we are not at ease with ourselves and with others. What seems to have happened is that we have all become producers and consumers with no generally agreed set of assumptions on theological, moral, ethical and spiritual values" (Mofid 2002, p. 4). The problem is greatly exacerbated by the fact that contemporary economics has "no systemic explanation of how the people in the underclass got where they are and how the system could be changed to raise them up" (de Soto 2000, p. 226). Contemporary economics is "a shambles", says Radford (2011):

> ... The problem is that the arguments are still going on. They have been for decades. No amount of point or counterpoint seems to resolve anything. Nor does evidence seem to matter much. Economics has become intellectual trench warfare that bursts into public view at

the most inappropriate times ... Patience is running out. It is time to do something. Society has skin in this game.

In any discussion of "where to from here" with respect to a rise in human happiness and freedom, use of the natural resource, land, must be given serious consideration. Land is not some stuff that antiquated agricultural peasants walked on. It is the primary element of need for mankind. Life is impossible without it. The need of access to "good and cheap" land today is the very same need of seventeenth and eighteenth century Americans. To verify the importance of the availability of land to an understanding of good economics, all that is needed is to read and understand the history of the settlement and establishment of America (and Australia, too – it is the same story); and take careful note of the importance of land to economic freedom. This importance has been spelled out by a rich vein of writers including Belloc (1936), Chesterton (1926), Steinbeck (1939) and Maugham (1944). "Widely distributed property as a condition of freedom is necessary to the normal satisfaction of human nature" (Belloc [1936] (2002), p. 27). A properly instituted land tax would ensure widely distributed property ownership, and the land tax is one of the oldest and least-disputed propositions in economic thought. Its underlying theory was developed at the beginning of the nineteenth century by the well-known and respected thinker, David Ricardo. Get the law of the land wrong and you've got *everything* wrong! Get the law of the land wrong and progress[30] and poverty will continue to march together; and though we might be a generous people in many respects, "when confronted with the no-man's-land of poverty we walk by on the other side" (Stewart 2008, p. 186). And so humankind is born into 'the promised land', with the promise being a life naturally endowed with justice, love, compassion and the common good; but which has instead been turned into the "current

---

[30] Economic growth.

wasteland" beset by individualism, self-interest, profit-maximisation, greed, godlessness, materialism and unethical behaviour (Mofid 2002, p. 70). Recent economic history, for many at least, has been a regression from promised land to wasteland, a descent to a state of being "untouched by the breath of god, unrestrained by human conscience".

In the end it comes down to the pitiful fact of wasted potential.

Look, no matter where you live, the biggest defect we human beings have is our short-sightedness. We don't see what we could be. We should be looking at our potential, stretching ourselves into everything we can become. But if you're surrounded by people who say "I want mine now", you end up with a few people with everything and a military to keep the poor ones from rising up and stealing it (Albom 1997, p. 156).

And now (mid-2020) we have:

Fear, an economy shut down, and a virus: what all this is teaching us about economics

Recent emergence of a virus has been accompanied by wide-spread fear that has led to the shut-down of whole economies. With the advent of shut-down and its accompanying social isolation has come clear demonstration of certain natural human propensities with respect to economics. These 'propensities' – four in particular – are always present (virus or no virus) but during 'normal' times are playing out without being noticed and, therefore, are taken for granted. In particular, the current fearful and 'closed' situation is revealing powerful human traits that bear directly on the everyday business of making a living and living together in peace and harmony.

These four propensities are:

(1) The importance of simple social contact

(2) The value to the human being of having something meaningful to do – every day of the working week

(3) The value of ordinary "diversions" from the business of making a living – sport in particular

(4) The importance, at the national level, of domestic *manufacturing* – particularly of essential goods and services

These four are now considered, in turn.

(1) The importance of simple social contact

In ordinary times simple social contact happens freely, 'automatically', but its value is not consciously appreciated. Appreciation of the real value of this human contact is made apparent only when it is cut off.

Every-day economic transactions – including buying a cup of coffee, shopping at the supermarket, buying a newspaper – embody human-to-human contact, and we human beings like that! It "nourishes" us, at a level deeper than the superficial. At the negative end of the spectrum of the feeling of being cut off is depression and suicide. This dreadful state of affairs is even showing up in school children being forced to stay at home rather than go to their 'workplace' (the classroom) (Aneeka Simonis, "Alarm at suicides", *Herald Sun*, Monday 4 May, p. 1). Social contact is simple, but it is important – necessary, in fact.

(2) The human value of having something meaningful to do, every day of the working week

As human beings we are creative and energetic (see chapter 5, *The special nature of work*). Also, we like to make a contribution – and I'm not talking here about monetary donations and the like – we like to feel that we are "doing our bit" in the community in which we live. The product of our work, which, importantly, includes the face-to-face interaction with the recipient, *is* that contribution. And the more we are deprived of the opportunity to work the greater is the sense of being cut-off, of being "left out", of being alone and impoverished, of not being able to make our contribution. For those deprived of employment, relief benefits do help, of course, "but for every physical symptom avoided, a mental toll has been exacted" (Catherine McGregor, *The Weekend Australian*, 2–3 May 2020, p. 22).

(3) The value to the human being of ordinary "diversions" from the business of making a living – sport in particular

This factor (the value of "diversions" from the business of making a living) is related closely to (2) above (the value of having something meaningful to do). But even for those who are gainfully employed in the normal sense of these words, "ordinary diversions" – sport in particular, gardening also – appear to have a very significant value in the community. Sport is a release for many from the tensions, frustrations and hassles of the daily job; gardening (a form of hobby) also, but it is a "creative outlet" as well – something of beauty is being created. Roger Sworder (1995) says of this:

"One of the most remarkable developments of the two centuries since the industrial revolution is the hobby. After working in the factory or the office people return home to practise in their periods of leisure what previously they would have done as work. This is the significance of gardening in a society which has mostly dis-pensed with agricultural labour, and of the millions of workshops in the backyards of suburban houses. Nothing could show more clearly than this that the old predispositions continue to exercise their sway over the personality, and they do so regardless of the fact that the work for which they fit us is no longer paid, nor other-wise rewarded than by the intrinsic satisfaction which it provides" (p. 123).

(4) The importance at the national level of domestic manufacturing – particularly of essential goods and services

The effect of the virus has shown us, graphically, the importance of having at least some control over the supply of essential goods and services. The alternative to having control is dependence, and dependence is weakness, particularly in the face of threats and difficulties and unexpected needs, all of which are part of human existence. In other words, reliance on somebody else for an essential good or service will, sooner or later, reveal a troublesome vulnerability that such reliance causes.

This is obvious, and yet we in this country have ignored this for a long time. This ignoring has been, largely, at the advice of 'expert economists' who preach the theoretical value of specialisation and trade (and who, by the way, have well-paid, protected jobs! – very different from the displaced workers put on the scrap-heap by the abandonment of industry and embrace of imports). There *is* value in specialisation and trade, but not for *everything*. Goods and services essential to basic survival are one major exception. "Australia needs to learn that free trade is for the biggest and least-cost producers. For everyone else it's a mug's game" (Craig Milne, *News Weekly*, 2 May 2020, p. 14).

Further: it seems absurd to have to be saying this – that we should be manufacturing essential goods – at a time when full employment of our people in meaningful jobs is *not* the rule. That is to say, there is an unwelcome level of unemployment; and surely it should not need to be said that the manufacture of essentials (at a **minimum**) is a fine opportunity to make meaningful employment more readily available to our otherwise unemployed people.

An economy is not "some nice, optional 'add-on'"

An economy is not some "nice idea", some "nice 'add-on'" to a supposed normal daily life. An economy is an essential part of "daily life", almost as important as breathing! Without an economy there is no life (in the everyday sense of this word) – and so "lock-downs" cannot go on forever. Permanent lockdown – which may save a number of lives from the health perspective – means no economic activity, no production of goods and services, no incomes with which to be able to buy them, and no inter-personal contact. An economy, perhaps surprisingly, is just *so* important! Our decision makers (in the bodily "health" realm) don't seem to understand this. Part of the reason for this apparent lack of understanding is that they all appear to have permanent, protected jobs and riskless weekly pay cheques. None of them appears to have lost a single cent as a consequence of community lock-downs (in fact, one senior state politician has reportedly pocketed a recent pay *rise* – of more than $40,000!). They don't appear to "get it"! Fortunately, there does appear to be one exception to this: our Prime Minister. He does seem to understand. "Prime Minister Scott Morrison has set a goal to restore a million jobs by opening up the economy as soon as Friday…school closures will cost 304,000 jobs, the controls on industry and public gatherings will lead to 708,000 lost jobs, and the slump in domestic and international demand will cost 516,000 jobs" (*The Age*, Wednesday 6 May 2020, p. 1).

But to return to the point of "a great disconnectedness": maybe, just maybe, the *real* problem, the *real* immediate concern is *philosophy* – specifically, the *lack of it* in the lives of individuals, communities and nations! "Perhaps what is distinctive about this world-epoch consists in *the closure of the dimension of the sacred*; perhaps *that* is the sole malignancy" (Heidegger 1993, p. 254). Allan Bloom wrote of "the closing of the American mind" in 1987 and today it appears that we are living in the midst of a hardening of the world's soul. In this "world-epoch" economists have hardened their souls and turned away from a consideration of what is sacred – human beings and their lives – and invented "false gods" as a substitute: exchange rates, interest rates, economic growth. To take just one example, Australian economic policy, upon the insistence of noisy economists who happen to have the ear of government, is obsessed with adherence to an exchange rate and international trade policy practised by few other countries in the world. The result is that whole industries (manufacturing in particular) have abandoned this country, leaving the lives of tens of thousands of its people in misery, including fear generated by the uncertainty of employment for those who still have a job. Similarly with interest rate policy: with an eye purely on a single number – the inflation rate – government has previously allowed interest rates to be increased to alarmingly-high levels, with harmful effects upon small business operators and mortgage holders and, from the perspective of manufacturers and exporters, very harmful effects upon the exchange rate. Today (July 2020) the interest rate is so low as to encourage unhealthy speculation in capital asset accumulation (particularly real estate) and at the same time so low as to deprive retirees of a decent income that they depend on now and had worked toward earlier in their life by making savings. And the same with economists' obsession with economic growth: the mantra seems to be, "never mind the hurtful effects upon the lives of those who do not benefit from growth, just set economic policy such that there *is* economic growth"! Said John Paul II: "Western culture is marked by the fatal attempt to secure the good of humanity by eliminating God" (Mofid, p. xiv). And with like sentiment Chief Rabbi Lord Sacks (2011, p. 14) says, "Those who believe that liberal democracy and the free market can be defended by the force of law and regulation alone, without an internalised sense of duty and morality, are tragically mistaken".

Contemporary economics has become stony-hearted. Economics has failed us; economics is continuing to fail us; and economics will go on failing us until it remembers its *purpose* as a subject, and puts first-principles first. Its purpose is to lift people's lives, to increase the well-being of humankind. Its first-principles are few in number, easy of understanding and simple to implement. To the detriment and frustration of countless millions, economists have put the consideration of people – their livelihoods and their sense of well-being – second, behind the promulgation and proliferation of clinically-neat and fancy theoretical concepts. Even something as simple, relevant and significant to people as the "basic wage" – that amount of money necessary for a man and his family to live on with some minimum degree of comfort – has long been abandoned by economists in favour of "market-driven" awards.

And so maybe the *real* immediate need is for a return to wisdom, with the starting point being a sincere question – three questions, in fact – on the part of the individual: *Why am I here? What am I supposed to be doing?* and *What should I be putting my values in?* "We put our values in the wrong things. And it leads to very disillusioned lives. I think we should talk about that" (Albom 1997, p. 123). And to facilitate answering these questions the wisdom of *good* economics[31] is essential, because economics has a great deal to do with how we live, and how we live has a vital influence upon shaping and realising (or not) our answers to the above three questions. Good economics talks about "the dignity of work" rather than "the cost of labour"; good economics recognises the importance of caring for "mother earth" and making access available to all who need her (which is everyone); and, most importantly, good economics embodies a firm and strong recognition of the public realm[32] and the endowment of public revenue which arises naturally in all economies. This revenue source is intended to meet the costs of the provision of public infrastructure, but in western democracies it is rarely collected for the public good. Instead there is a reliance on taxes of various kinds to pay for public expenditures. Failure to collect the public revenue for public expenditure

---

[31] Not the impoverished, corrupted version peddled by the unthinking majority of today's economists.

[32] Enunciated by Donald Lambie (2019). The 'public realm' is distinct from but works in conjunction with the private realm. To take the simplest of examples, when a homeowner turns on the garden tap to water the vegetables, the provision of water is a public service (and so is of the 'public realm'); the efforts of the gardener in planting, weeding, and otherwise growing the vegetables is of the 'private realm'. To take another example: with respect to the retail industry, the economic value of the presence of the buying public and all the facilities that are needed to smooth the way for this presence (of large numbers of shoppers) – including roads, streets, footpaths, security – is of the 'public realm'.

purposes – and thereby allowing the price of land to escalate to heights unaffordable for many wanting to establish a home – is the reason for the significant advances of the western world along the lines of immense and startling economic progress running hand-in-hand with increasingly widespread and miserable poverty.

The wise, the true philosophers, say that the reason for the disconnectedness evident in the economic world of today is that people have become disconnected from *themselves*, disconnected from the truth of their own being. And the economic conditions – the laws relating to the economic realm – that most people live under are a major cause of this sense of disconnectedness. (It is difficult – very difficult – to be in memory of the truth of one's being if living under conditions of poverty and deprivation). This is why Donald Lambie (2019) says that good economics is "not really very different at all from what we understand by philosophy". The aim of philosophy, and the real aim of human life, is to facilitate full remembering of the truth of our own being; and how we live has a deep and profound effect on how we come to regard our own true being. Together with philosophy, in fact as part of it, economic law has a major effect on how we live. Good economic law embodies wisdom the purpose of which is to *illuminate* how we live. And human life is meant to be lived happily and in freedom. Hence, economics is not really very different from philosophy. We need to talk about that!

REFERENCES

Abjorensen, Norman 1993, *John Hewson: a Biography*, Lothian Books, Sydney

Albom, Mitch 1997, *Tuesdays with Morrie*, Hodder, Sydney

Anderson, Phillip J 2008, *The Secret Life of Real Estate: how it moves and why*, Shepheard-Walwyn, London

Bhagavad Gita 2000, *Hodgkinson trans.*, John Scottus School, Dublin Ireland

Belloc, Hilaire [1936] 2002, *The Restoration of Property*, IHS Press, Norfolk

Bird, Paul 2011, *Herald Sun*, 5 April, p. 10, Melbourne

Bloom, Allan 1987, *The Closing of the American Mind*, Simon & Schuster, New York

Brown, William 2011, *"How shall we protect the wages of the weak"? Insights*, Melbourne Business and Economics, vol. 10, November, pp. 5 - 9, University of Melbourne

Chesterton, GK 2001 (1926), *The Outline of Sanity*, IHS Press, Norfolk

Churchill, Winston 1909, *Winston Churchill said it all better than we can*, Edinburgh lecture; reported 2010 in Churchill Edinburgh website www.landvaluetax.org/current-affairs-comment/winston-churchill-said-it-all-better

Day, Philip 1995, *Land: the elusive quest for social justice, taxation reform & a sustainable planetary environment*, Australian Academic Press, Brisbane Australia

De Soto, Hernando 2000, *The Mystery of Capital: Why Capitalism Triumphs in the West and Fails Everywhere Else*, Black Swan, London

Emerson, Ralph Waldo [1841] 1982, *Selected Essays*, Penguin Books, New York

Evans-Pritchard, Ambrose 2011, *The Business Age*, 11 January, Melbourne

Fraser, Malcolm & Margaret Simons 2010, *Malcolm Fraser: The Political Memoirs*, Miegunyah Press, Melbourne

Gaffney, Mason & Fred Harrison 1994, *The Corruption of Economics*, Shepheard-Walwyn, London

Galbraith, JK 2010, quoted in Michael Hudson, "The Counter-Enlightenment: Its Economic Program – and the Classical Alternative", *Progress*, Autumn, p. 15, Melbourne

George, Henry [1879] 1992, *Progress and Poverty* (Centennial Edition), Robert Schalkenbach Foundation, New York

George, Henry [1879] 1979, Commemoration of the Centenary of *Progress and Poverty*, Department of Economics, University of Sydney

Hamilton, C & R Denniss 2005, *Affluenza: when too much is never enough*, Allen & Unwin, Sydney

Harrison, Fred 2005, *Boom Bust: house prices, banking and the depression of 2010*, Shepheard-Walwyn, London

Heidegger, Martin 1993, *Basic Writings*, ed. by David Krell, Routledge, UK

Henry Review (The) 2010, *Australia's future tax system*, http://taxreview. treasury.gov.au

Herald Sun 2011, "Findings released by Britain's Home Office and Ministry of Justice", 26 October, p. 23, Melbourne

Hill, Malcolm 1999, *"Enemy of Injustice: the Life of Andrew MacLaren"*, Othila Press, London

Hyde, Joseph 2001, *Annual economics lecture*, School of Economic Science, Hinde Street Methodist Church, London

Johnson, Paul 1997, *A History of the American People*, Harper Perennial, New York

Jones, Barry 1982, *Sleepers Wake!* Oxford University Press

Keynes, JM 1933, *The Means to Prosperity*, Macmillan, London (quoted in *News Weekly*, 8 August 2009, p. 5)

Kolakowski, Leszek 2009, *News Weekly*, 8 August, Melbourne

Kwitney, Jonathan 1997, *Man of the Century: The Life and Times of Pope John Paul II*, Henry Holt and Company, New York

Lambie, Donald, unpublished address to the School of Philosophy and Economic Science, London, September 2019

Landes, David 1999, *The Wealth and Poverty of Nations*, Abacus, Harvard, US

MacLaren, Leon 1943, *Nature of Society*, School of Economic Science, London

MacLaren, Leon 1993, *MacLaren Lectures,* vol. 2 (16 September), Cape Town, South Africa

McFarlane, Ian 2011, *News Weekly,* 12 November, Melbourne

McInerney, Monica 2006, *Odd One Out,* Penguin, London

Mahabharata (Kisari Mohan Ganguli) 1997 edition, Munshiram Manoharlal Publishers, New Delhi

Makewell, Raymond 2001, *Economic Wisdom,* pp. 139-141 (Plato, *Laws*) (Economic Wisdom, p. 139) [Economic Wisdom (EW), pp. 127-142 (Plato)] (*Laws* 736, 740, 743, 744)

Mann, Tom 1979, *"Tom Mann's memoirs",* quoted in Commemoration of the Centenary of Publication of Progress and Poverty, Australian School of Social Science, Sydney

Mason, Ian 2007, *The Transformation of Economics: Natural Law, Economics and the Great Jurisprudence,* recorded lecture, (13 November), Hinde Street Methodist Church, London

Maugham, W Somerset [1944] 2000, *The Razor's Edge,* Vintage, London

Meek, Ronald L 1962, *The Economics of Physiocracy,* Augustus Kelley Publishers (1993 reprint), US

Mirrlees, J. et al. 2011, "The Taxation of Land and Property", *Tax by Design: the Mirrlees Review,* Oxford University Press); (www.ifs.org.uk)

Mofid, Kamran 2002, *Globalisation for the Common Good,* Shepheard-Walwyn, London

Mueller, John D 2010, *Redeeming Economics,* Intercollegiate Studies Institute, London

Radford, Peter 2011, *"Ethics in Economics – Where Is It?"* real-world economics review, issue 58, 2-8, 12 December (www.paecon.net/PAERReview/issue58Radford58.pdf)

Rajan, Raghuram 2010, *Fault Lines,* Princeton University Press

Reagan, Ronald 1990, *An American Life,* Simon and Schuster, US

Ruskin, John 2011, in *News Weekly,* 29 October, p. 13, Melbourne

Sacks, Chief Rabbi Lord 2011, "Has Europe lost its Soul?" in *News Weekly,* 3 March 2012, Freedom Publishing, Melbourne

Schwartz, Steven 2011, "Universities dispensing knowledge without wisdom", in *News Weekly,* 29 October, Melbourne

Shankaracharya 2003, *Tradition* booklet (16 April), Melbourne

Steinbeck, John 1939, *Grapes of Wrath,* Viking Press, New York

Stewart, John 2008, *The President,* Shepheard-Walwyn, London

Stewart, John 2001, *Standing for Justice: a biography of Andrew MacLaren MP,* Shepheard-Walwyn, London

Sworder, Roger, Mining, Metallurgy and the Meaning of Life, Quakers Hill Press, 1995

Teese, Colin 2012, "The case against floating exchange rates" in *News Weekly,* 17 March, Melbourne

Thoreau [1906] 1951, *Journal,* Houghton Mifflin Co., Boston

Tisdell, 1972, *Microeconomics: The Theory of Economic Allocation,* p. 45; quoted in "Economics and university life: further reflections and experiences of Clem Tisdell", *International Journal of Social Economics,* 2000, 27, 7/8/9/10, p. 22.

Trengove, Alan 1969, *John Grey Gorton: an informal biography,* Cassell Australia

Vivekananda, Swami 2009 (1947), *Work and Its Secret,* Advaita Ashrama, Calcutta

Wolfensohn, James D. 2010, *A Global Life,* Pan Macmillan, Sydney

Wright, Ronald 2004, *A Short History of Progress,* Da Capo Press, Cambridge MA

Young, John 1996, *The Natural Economy,* Shepheard-Walwyn, London

Index